Changes of the Heart

With chapters by

Karen Allen
Alina Bas
Holly Berman
Dee Carrell
Amy Johnson
Mary Ann Lowry
Polly O'Connor
Anna Paradox
Jo Pillmore
Erin Postle
Ned Rios
Valerie LaPenta Steiger
Roma Strong Zanders

Edited by

Anna Paradox

With a Foreword by Dr. Martha Beck

Foreword

I've been a "life coach" for well over a decade. For the first two years, I had no idea what to call this thing I did: it was a little like therapy, but not for the mentally ill; a little like career counseling, but not for people who mistake their careers for their lives. I never dreamed that other people were doing the same thing, or something similar, until I read in a magazine that life coaching was the latest American fad. It was a little like patching together a few rags to make a serviceable garment, and finding out it fit in perfectly with the latest trends at New York Fashion Week. Who knew?

Five years ago, at this writing, I began training other life coaches. The original training model was a marathon: three days of intense connection between small groups of coach cadets, everyone learning and practicing various coaching tools on one another, connecting more intensely with one another – and with me – than seemed altogether prudent. Then I'd launch these new coaches into their careers, feeling like a heartless mother bird who'd given her chicks only 72 hours to grow wings before expecting them to fly.

After they'd gone, I often worried about my new coaches. Had they really internalized the tools? Had I demanded too much of them intellectually and emotionally? What would happen to them when they had their first nightmare client, their first crisis of confidence, their first nightmare in which scores of clients dressed as the Dallas Cowboy Cheerleaders attacked them with fondue forks? Sometimes I'd worry about them as a group, sometimes as individuals.

Clearly, I needed a life coach.

How fortunate that I'd trained some!

Whenever I encounter my coaches in Real Life, I am stunned by their ability to give me great advice. Their kindness, intelligence, and insight calms me down and cheers me up. I still don't know what they see in me, but what I see in them is a true vocation for helping others experience more joy and less suffering. I pushed each of them to find a personal voice and point of interest. The best of them took that advice and ran with it. The evidence of that is right in your hands.

Each of the authors represented in this collection has added her own particular experience, research, and expertise to the basic "toolkit" we all use in our coaching. As I read their work, I found myself taking notes, underlining, and stopping to try the exercises. Guess what? They work. These are some smart and committed coaches, and if you grapple with any of the issues addressed in their essays, you'll find yourself breathing more easily as you read, knowing that someone has been lost in the same wilderness you're traveling – and found a way out.

I became a coach by standing on the shoulders of giants: Byron Katie, who is mentioned approximately 500 times a day by me and each of my coaches; ACT Therapy as created by Steven Hayes, Russ Harris, and others; the whole vanguard of positive psychologists and social cognitive neuroscientists who've recently revolutionized our cultural understanding of human behavior. I'm no giant, and there's not much strength in my shoulders, but I'm honored and grateful that the authors of this book have gotten a little lift from our Tribe of coaches. I hope that many readers can be blessed by their connection to these authors, as I am every day.

Martha Beck

For Martha Beck

Your teachings gave us the foundation for the work we love: life coaching.

We would also like to thank:
Our editor, Anna Paradox, who guided this project from vision to print;

And our clients – you give our work meaning.

Table of Contents

Introduction

What if every challenge you face could lead you back to your heart?

That is the promise of Martha Beck life coaching.

This book can help you solve life's problems. There are tools here for easier parenting, choosing more rewarding careers, losing weight, overcoming grief, and more. Even better, every one of these chapters will help you find the solutions that align your life with the wisdom and desires inside you. We're talking about creating a life that uniquely suits you – not the one your teachers recommended, or what that guy you met while walking the dog said, or what the deodorant commercials on TV say you should want. Your life – the life that feels free and joyful and completely aligned with your essential self – that's what these tools build. These chapters are gentle guideposts to changes of the heart, and changes from the heart.

Thirteen coaches, trained and certified by Martha Beck, wrote the chapters of this book. Each of us chose a challenge that attracted her essential self. We included tools that you can use right away to improve your life. Each coach put her own experience and her own insights into her chapter.

Because that's what it's all about – each of us sharing our strategies for overcoming the challenges you face.

What does it mean to be a Martha Beck Life Coach?

Each one of the coaches in this book responded to the teachings of Martha Beck. We were drawn to her wisdom and her humor. Her concepts – like the Essential Self (a core part of each person's being that holds their unique strengths and desires) and Turtle Steps (making progress one small action at a time) – make sense to us. We answered a call: each of us said, "Yes. I want to help people discover their authentic lives, the way Martha does." We trained with her, learned her tools, and received certification in her methods.

And each of us is different. Following our own hearts, we have each turned our attention to the areas of life that most interest us. Starting from the foundation of Martha's huge collection of techniques, we have learned more tools, made variations on her tools and others, and created our own. There is one tool we refer to most often – The Work of Byron Katie®. There is nothing better for peeling away the illusions that cover your real self. Find Katie's original version at www.thework.com – we recommend it.

We have gone down the paths that life presented to us – now each of us can turn back to you and call, "We made it across that rough patch! This is what the path ahead is like, and here are some ways to make it easier."

Each of us offers coaching in her own way. We've put our contact information at the end of our chapters. Look there for access to blogs, newsletters, other free resources, and our individual coaching services. It is our true desire to help you through life's journey.

There is a magnetic attraction to people who are living from their authentic self. Such people look comfortable in their skin. They approach each day with the joy of choosing their own path. Even when they face difficult times, they operate from a core of peace. You can become like them, as you use these tools to live through your own changes of the heart. Each challenge can become a gift that opens you to new strengths and new discoveries.

These coaches give me that sense of peace. It has been a pleasure to spend time with them as we created these gifts for you. I enjoyed their company, and I know you will, too.

Anna Paradox

You've Just Been Elected to The Board

Direct Your Life Like A Million Dollar Business

by Jo Pillmore

Carole and I are talking about her nursing job. She enjoys her job, but she doesn't want to do it the rest of her life. "I've got regular hours with good pay, but I feel like I'm on a Merry-Go-Round that has no off switch. Go to work, come home and rest, just to go to work again. I see other people out there living their lives while I keep circling with the horses. I'd like to try some new things. But how am I ever gonna get off this thing? And when I do get off, what do I do then?" she asks. "I mean, at least, I know who I am on this ride. What if I get off and I fail? Then what do I do?"

Jim is on another carnival ride but stuck just the same. His job is commission-based and has him up high on the Ferris Wheel of life with great sales one month and rewarding himself with trips to the mall, only to circle back down with no sales the next two months, scraping for the mortgage payments.

And then the call comes from Sheila, "That's it. We got the notice today they're downsizing 50 people in my department. I'll be lined up to Timbuktu at the unemployment office, going in and out of interviews for months, if I'm lucky to get interviewed at all. Now what?"

Yes, my friends, tighten your belts and hold on tight, this is definitely a motion sickness moment. All this talk of circling around, weaving in and out, and reeling up and down is starting to make me dizzy. No wonder people are confused about what to do next. These people tell me they feel like they're spinning out of control. But the reality is – they're motionless. Stuck in the same place, month after month, that turns into year after year.

I hear this a lot from my clients. They've worked hard; gone to school; got the job, but now what? Some are at the point where they are ready for a change while others may have change forced upon them from a downward economy, ailing parents, or kids heading to college. Some, like Carole, are just miserable and they don't know why.

No matter what your situation is right now – changing careers, unhappy with your life, looking for a new job – before you start your next life phase, you have to know where you're coming from. Time to call a Board of Directors Meeting – and you are the Big Kahuna!

We plan for a lot of things: our vacations, our next car purchase, the best gym to join, the weekend; heck we even plan what we want to have for breakfast the next day. (With some subliminal nudges. Or have you not noticed the after 9PM TV ads for delicious jumbo breakfast platters?) But we rarely plan how we want our lives and relationships to be.

When was the last time you actually sat down and made plans for your life? Think about that. I mean really give it a few minutes of thought. I'll wait.

If you're like a lot of people that I've asked that question of, the answer would be "Uh. . . when I talked to my high school guidance counselor?" We get the job or become involved in a relationship and then just let go of the reins, cross our fingers, and hope for the best. So why not give our Life as much attention in planning as we do the gazillions of business, club, or school meetings we've attended?

Now, understand, I am not talking about a Carved-in-Stone-Never-to-Waver-From plan. The kind of plan I'm talking about is one that gives us knowledge about who we are and where we are right now. It's a plan to build from. It's a plan that will support our dreams.

If your Life was a company that you owned, would you be treating it the same way you do now? Would you ignore the money it creates and spends? Would you pay attention to it only when it was in trauma – like a robbery, or an employees' strike? Would you have no clue where it's going to be next year, five years, or ten years from now? Hmmmm, I'm guessin' that would be a big N-O. As a business owner, you would know your cash flow, you'd be tweaking your product line and planning new products or services. You'd be dreaming of new places and goals to take your company and projecting your growth not annually but quarterly! So why short change your own Life?

Let's take a little time to see your self (and your partner if applicable) in this same light of importance. Let's imagine your Life as a Company and you as the all powerful Directors on the Board. Impressive already, isn't it? And since this Company can't (nor should it) be allowed to run itself, it's time to call a Board of Directors Meeting.

GETTING AWAY:

Typically, high end Board Directors are whisked off to luxury accommodations for their annual Directors Meeting. One thing for sure, they certainly aren't figuring out next year's Operating Budget in the kitchen on the back of an old envelope between baby feedings. And there's a good reason for this: Focus. The Directors need to get away from distractions so they can focus on the Meeting.

So I suggest my clients plan their own get-away meeting. This could be held over the weekend at a hotel, either out of town or locally. (Tip: Lots of business hotel chains lower their weekend prices because most of their clientele leave town Friday through Monday. These hotels are usually very nice, quiet, and offer nice perks like free breakfasts.) If a hotel's not possible maybe you could barter with a friend or family member to stay at your house (and babysit if need be) while you hold your meeting at their house.

Before the Directors fly off to their Board Meeting, they'll be given a synopsis of how the Company is doing, its assets and liabilities, its needs both present and projected, and its plans for the future. You want to be just as prepared. Here are some suggestions to get you started:

1. **Financials:** How can you get anywhere unless you first know where you're coming from? Take this moment to find the big "You Are Here" arrow in your Life. Where you are coming from is important to help you get to where you want to be, my friend. So gather up the basics of where you are right now: all your assets – the money coming in; and your liabilities – where the money is going. List your monthly cost of living

expenses. (Tip: There's a free worksheet download to help you organize this at www.jopillmore.com) This is "Show Me the Money" time. You want to be truthful but not complicated. Make sure you have all the information and it's in a format that is easy for you to understand. If you keep in the back of your head the Board Director metaphor, you can more easily detach from the personal part of the finances to make it user friendly.

2. **Be Prepared:** Here are some tools you may want to bring: a calculator, laptop, paper, pens, maybe a financial reference book that can answer questions, and a spiral notebook for the minutes and notes. The notebook is important. It is what you'll leave with and refer to during the year. Oh! And a swimsuit. A lot of these places have great Jacuzzis.

3. **Dreaming:** Before you go to your meeting, you should spend a bit of time thinking about some ideas you've had about your future. Even the crazy idea you had last year about where you'd like to be in 20 years. Just think about them for sharing at the Meeting. Gather up all your hopes and dreams and pack them too.

The Meeting

Friday night, check into your room and relax. Maybe have a nice meal, even take a walk or a soak in the Jacuzzi (I told you business hotels have great perks!) and just enjoy yourself. Bringing some fun to the process helps you relax for the next day. Saturday morning, get the coffee perking and bring breakfast to your room. This is a working breakfast. Start your meeting.

IN THE CLEAR LIGHT OF DAY:

Now is the time to go over your information so you understand where the money is and what you need monthly to survive. Record your information in your notebook. Even though one person may handle the bills and finances, it is important that each Board Director understands:

1. How much money comes in and from what sources
2. How much money goes out – where and why.

For some of us, this will be a difficult piece of the meeting. If you are the one who pays the bills, have patience with the one that doesn't and vice versa. Maybe your 401(k) isn't as big as you thought or maybe you've spent a lot more than you planned. But in the clear light of Saturday morning's sunshine, breathe deep and go from where you are right now. Financial Goddess Suze Orman wisely says *"The first, and most difficult step is to absolve yourself and your spouse or partner of any guilt . . . agree that the past is past, and we are going to focus on the future. Whatever mistakes you feel you have made with money. . . are irrelevant. We are free to move forward only when we remove the emotional shackles of regret."*

Now you should have a solid understanding of your income and expenses. Some of you are feeling pretty good, seeing that you are in better shape than you thought. And some of you may be reaching for the aspirin or antacids or both. But don't stop now; this next step is important. Well, unless you are the recent happy winner of the Tri-State Power Ball. If that's true, I say drinks for everybody and you're paying! Seriously, by doing this piece you'll see that your finances play a big part in how you move forward in your life. Be brave. Push forward to this next step, because this is where you start gaining your Power.

THINK TANK:

Many Board Directors are also members of Think Tanks. Think Tank consultants are problem solvers. They see the problem as just that: a problem that needs solving. They make no judgments or complaints or criticisms. Did we buy too many Widgets when we sold more Wadgets? Okay, let's crunch some numbers and find the best way to solve that problem. For you, the Think Tank problems may look more like this:

- If I want to save for Junior to go to college what should I do now?
- How can I pay down credit card debt?
- Now that John has lost his job, what do we need to do?
- With housing prices down, what's the best way to buy a new house?
- What would it cost to get a Master's degree?
- How can I save more money and live for less?
- Where do I want to invest my savings to prepare for early retirement?
- How can I turn my hobby into a moneymaker?

Try to detach your view as if it were a business situation, just like a Think Tank consultant. If you feel yourself getting nervous or emotional, write down what makes you afraid and then write in your notebook small steps that you can do to feel just a little better about it. Writing it down will keep your Mind from spinning the problem into a Titanic size disaster. (Go to the website for help.) And remember as you share that fear, it is a fear based on how you see things. Laying blame on someone else may make you feel righteous but stalls out the forward moving process. Read the Suze Orman quote again and *really* mean it this time.

Why is this part so important? Because when it comes to change, many people make obstacles in their life based on what they *think* they know about their finances. It can be one of the biggest excuses people use for not trying new things in their lives.

As in:

I/We can't afford to:

- Live on one salary
- Go back to school and finish my degree
- Buy a second home
- Take off and be home with the kids for a year
- Try a new career on an entry level salary
- Take a sabbatical and write the Great American Novel
- Go part time so I can help my parents now that Daddy is ill
- Retire early
- Travel
- Have a baby
- Get another degree
- Spend more time with my grandkids
- Go work for a year in the Peace Corps (Yes, it is still around!)

When you read some of the things above, is there something that tugs on you? Something that is a piece of a dream or a plan you've had? These "I Can't" thoughts are common problems that we've all experienced. The tug of war is between what Martha Beck calls the Social Self and the Essential Self – the choices you made based on what others thought or said to you, instead of what you really wanted for yourself. Look inside yourself to see what excuse you may be using. Write them in your notebook and recognize that it's an excuse. Not reality.

It's good to start looking at this now because many ideas may be time sensitive, based on how old you are or especially around your family. Once your kids are grown, there are no trips available in the Way Back Machine. And trust me, when it comes to children, this maxim is true: "The days are long, but the years are short." You can't get back the time you dreamed of spending with family, whether it's your children or your parents. Many people have worked out a system that juggles things out really well to have the best of both. If this is a desire for you, now is the time to give it serious thought.

Here's another question to ask yourself: "If I added up all the hours I work (including the hours I think about work) and divide my paycheck by those realtime hours, what would I be earning per hour?" Is that hourly wage worth it to avoid your dreams? What could you do to make that better? (Tip: A great book that really puts all this life value into perspective is: *Your Money or Your Life* by Joe Dominguez and Vicki Robins.)

Many obstacles keep people from reaching their dreams. I've seen some of my clients create a subconscious barrier with their money (or lack of it) to keep themselves from trying something new with their lives. Some people actually could afford their ideas or dreams, they just didn't know it. Others tell themselves they can't try something new because they have to keep toiling away for The Man. "I have to keep working this dead-end soul-destroying job because I'm in too much debt." But for a lot of us, it wasn't The Man that put us here. What put us here was not paying attention to the money that we earned and the way we spent it. It's an excuse, and I'm not even going to call it a good one. It's just an excuse.

Then there are other people who get in debt or overspend to feel better about themselves, like the exhilaration of shopping and buying, say, a new 150 inch plasma TV (yes, there is such a thing!) or the top of the line cell phone for your 4 year old (well he's so cute and he likes to play with it!). These can temporarily block out the thoughts that you don't like your job or your life situation. But the keyword here is: temporarily.

For some, this lifestyle is like a call and response cheer. The boss yelled at you today for no good reason, so you start looking for the latte and Danish cart. You had to work late again last night, but Saturday you're going to buy your son that video game. Maybe two! For a few fleeting moments of distraction, you feel better. But just for a moment.

Observe what you're doing right now in your Life and discuss how you'd like to handle things in the future. If you see huge outgo and less income, now is the time to make suggestions on how to adjust it. If you're doing really well, write down ideas to get more out of your money and your Life. Write everything down in the notebook and find steps to make it better.

I know going over the finances is scary, but I always suggest my clients do the financial piece first because you have to know where you are to get to where you want to go. Stay in Think Tank mode until you feel you have solid plans to get your finances under control.

If you think you may fall in the spending denial categories, WAKE UP!! Now is your chance to get it together. Be *glad* you are looking at this now and preparing to take the next right step in controlling your life. Forgive yourself and start living a conscious Life based on your own choices.

By now you should have covered a large piece of the Meeting. You've done a good job of seeing the present state. You've acknowledged the high points and low ones. In your Think Tank, you've really been problem solving and hopefully have either a game plan or assigned steps for a better game plan. Now is the time to unpack your dreams and ideas for the Future.

THE MASTERMIND GROUP:

The Future is defined as events that will or are likely to happen in a time yet to come. I do like the sound of that: **Events that will happen or are likely to happen.** It's time for you to start saying these events out loud.

You've come to the fun and most daring part of the Meeting. People in MasterMind groups are the type of people that are paid big bucks to NOT color inside the lines. They are known for their ability to dream big, to dare to try new things. They are fearless in their thinking because they know that no idea is too stupid to say out loud. Did you get that part? No idea is too stupid to say out loud. Where would Steve Jobs or George Lucas or Oprah be now if they hadn't started dreaming out loud? This is where you become the MasterMind of your own Life.

Working as a MasterMind has a major distinction from being in the Think Tank. In the Think Tank, you were problem solving and you created designated steps to answer your specific problems or needs. As a MasterMind, it's more important to figure out *where* you want to be in the Future and see yourself there – than to dwell on a step-by-step detailed outline of how you want to get there. So, why am I saying you shouldn't get really precise with plans and timelines about how to achieve these dreams? Because too many details will restrict creative options and discourage growth.

I tell my clients that our Minds are like search engines – like Google. Tell Google what you are looking for and it will find it for you, and in a zillion different ways. (Who knew canned SPAM had flavors and that they love it in Hawaii and Guam??)

Tell your Mind what you are looking for, and your Mind, just like Google, will get the information for you and in a lot of different ways. For example, ever wanted a new car, say a shiny blue sports convertible? Ooooo! Shiny!! Once you start thinking about it, what happens next? Suddenly, like magic, it's everywhere. It starts passing you on the freeway, parking two rows beside you in the parking lot, showing up behind you in the car pool line. Where was it before you wanted it? Yep, pal, it was always there. You just didn't tell your Mind it was important, so it deleted it.

Telling our Mind we want more information about some-thing sends it, just like Google, all over *our* world giving us lots of different options to Make It So Number One. Many could be options that you may never have thought about before. But if you make a rigid detailed format of how your idea must come true, your Mind might delete important options that could have gotten you to your goal easier and sooner. That's why you want to be flexible for your Mind to bring you options.

Say one of your ideas is to turn what is now your hob-by into a money-making career. Just talking and writing about it in the Meeting will give it importance to your Mind. Then as you think about how fun that would be, your Mind will artfully start nudging you towards books, billboards, magazine articles, shops. Or you start chatting about it to a friend who it turns out knows someone who does that for a living. Coincidence? I don't think so. Your Mind is on a roll and once it brings you the options, then you can move forward as you want and at your own pace.

If you make detailed plans of how and when you will create the career, your Mind may delete important options. Or you may start getting frustrated that it's not happening by your time chart and then give up on the idea all together. MasterMinds feel good about their new ideas and let the Mind bring them choices. That's why I encourage clients not only to visualize but daydream about their ideas as if they already exist. This gives the Mind a deeper understanding and keeps you feeling good.

Where do you see yourself next year? In five years? What will be the status of your life? What do you want to do in your life and in your relationship? For instance, do you really want to move to a bigger city (or the country) and how would that look and feel? This is a place where all those random ideas you've been thinking can now come into play. (Tip: I've got some ideas to help jumpstart you at my website.)

Write out your plans and dreams for yourself. Really. Go ahead. Dream BIG! Think wide open with no holds barred.

KNOW THAT YOU KNOW:

One of the most powerful beliefs Martha shared with us in our training was that everyone knows deep inside what is right for them, but sometimes life gets in the way. That's what I love about coaching, helping people get back to that moment of knowing.

This is the time to give your self permission to think like a MasterMind, going deep inside your heart and setting your imagination free. Be fearless in your thinking. Remember that ideas come in all sizes, from taking water-color classes to traveling through Europe for a year. . . or two. Bring up new dreams and honor the ones you've carried in your heart for years. Many times the strongest ideas aren't new. Have fun thinking and talking about what the dreams and ideas might look like now and in the future. Capture them in your notebook. Writing in the notebook helps give new ideas a holding place and a sense of importance. Even feel free to take this MasterMind part on a walk or to dinner. That may bring up even more creative ideas. Tell your Mind the dreams and ideas that are important to you. Then let your Mind help show you the way.

MEETING ADJOURNED:

This Directors exercise is challenging and powerful. I've witnessed some astonishing Life changes with my clients just from this one weekend. At evening's end, you can rest knowing the Meeting is done. You've really done some amazing work. No, it wasn't easy, but I'm betting you have a better idea of what you want from your Life than you've had in a long time. Because now you know where you are and once you do, you can go anywhere!

Jo Pillmore came intuitively to coaching by working on her own life. She has studied with many teachers including Martha Beck, Abraham-Hicks, Byron Katie, and Gary Zukav. She is also a certified hypnosis and NLP Practitioner. Jo believes that everyone has within them all the resources they need to be, do, and have what they want. Coaching can help you gain access to these resources. Jo's coaching is based on a simple concept that only you know what is right for you. In coaching, there's no judgment, no looking deep into the past, it's just looking at right now, finding where you want to be and getting there. For more information: www.jopillmore.com

Please see bibliography on p. 257.

Please see bibliography on p. 257.

ೞ

The Gift of Raising Challenging Children

by Holly Berman

I clearly remember the moment when I realized that I was in over my head as a mother. My first-born, a daughter, had been energetic even in utero. Her exuberant and charming personality helped balance the more difficult parts of her character. However, I was caught short by this statement when she was in 2nd grade: "Mom, sometimes I just want to throw myself in front of a car and kill myself." What to make of that? Is this part of her ongoing drama or something that deserved more investigation?

To start, I asked other mothers of kids her age, "Has your child ever said anything like this?" Their peculiar looks told me even more than their measured denials. Those looks! Any mother of a "challenging child" gets to know them well. Even for someone who tends to be pretty secure, it is hard not to feel the judgment behind the looks and to internalize some painful thoughts about them.

Frankly, I couldn't blame parents of non-challenging children for those looks. I might have done the same if the roles were reversed. Having children is the ultimate roll of the dice. There are your preconceived expectations, and then there is the reality. Martha Beck writes movingly in *Expecting Adam* of her shock at learning her unborn child had Down's Syndrome. Life for her and her family would never be the same. For her and for me, our challenging children led us to unanticipated places. Ultimately, we both used those experiences to become life coaches and help others on their journeys through the unknown.

Shortly after that second grade inquiry, we began seeing a series of therapists as a family. Approximately every 3 years, we'd see someone new for a short period, hoping for better advice to make life with our challenging child more peaceful. If you are on this road, you know that helpful advice is very, very difficult to find, even in big cities. Two other scenes stand out in my mind.

My daughter, a sophomore in high school, is meeting with her psychiatrist. I am in the waiting room. Despite the white noise machine designed to mask any conversations, I can clearly hear the doctor screaming at my child in frustration. Two thoughts occurred simultaneously: 1) At least this proves that my child can push anyone's buttons, so I can't be all that bad a mom; and 2) Shouldn't a therapist be able to control their emotional frustration better than me?

I drop my daughter off at a therapeutic boarding school in rural Vermont for her junior year. She cries, "Don't leave me. I'll change and be good." I leave her behind, drive to a national forest site nearby, pull over in the rental car, find a good spot to sit on the ground and sob.

It is possible to come through challenges like these. This is who my daughter is today:

- a beautiful, energetic, creative, talented 25 year old
- who has lived in Thailand and Scotland,
- who is braver than most anyone I know,
- who has a degree in documentary film-making

- who appears as an extra in the movie, *Stranger Than Fiction* (walking past the guitar store that Will Ferrell will frequent),
- who flew around the US working on a documentary on Goths who take cruises,
- who started her own business, creating personal video biographies,
- who lives happily at home, with parents she describes as the best in the world.

Her journey and mine have been intertwined. Her needs forced me to grow. Without the challenges that she provided, my life would be flatter and emptier. Recognizing that the parts of her that drove me nuts were the parts of myself that I "rejected" was the first step toward my creating a better life. Learning to listen to my heart, to truly feel my emotions, to allow myself to be vulnerable, and to acknowledge mistakes created the space for us to connect on a meaningful level. Yoga and meditation practices helped provide more serenity and clarity. Life Coach training with Martha Beck supercharged the process with powerful tools that transformed the way I approach every day.

What does it mean to be a "challenging child?" Other authors/therapists have used the words "spirited" or "difficult." As I noted above, raising my daughter was a challenge in every sense of the word. If I said the sky was blue, she said it was grey. Almost every thing could turn into a battle. It was not until I shifted my own thought process that we were able to experience true communication and loving concern that went both ways. I came to see that the *challenge* called for changes in my own thought patterns and expectations.

There are categories in the psychiatrist's bible, the DSM: Oppositional Defiant Disorder, Borderline Personality

Disorder, ADD, ADHD, etc. The worlds of insurance reimbursement and Special Education services – areas I don't plan to address in this brief chapter – require these labels. But, when you're caught up in familial chaos, the categories are meaningless. Your child's problems are uniquely his/her own. These labels are powerful, though, because the very words you use to describe and define the problem do carry weight as they translate into thoughts, emotions, and actions.

In working with mothers of challenging children, I focus on the definition of "the problem," and its effects on their own self-esteem. In my workshops, mothers express their pain in words like these:

"I am a failure as a mom. I cannot believe that I acted that way."

"I cannot believe I said those words."

"I want my child to love me and to know that I love him/her."

Often they cry with relief at being in a safe place with people who understand intimately. I like the term "challenging children" for a specific reason. Yes, the personalities of these children could be trying to any parent. However, some combinations seem designed to present particular challenges, like that experienced by a parent who likes order and punctuality who has a child who likes chaos and is a born procrastinator. This example describes one of my ongoing issues with my daughter. My tendency is to hide my emotions (some might say bury them); she is upfront with whatever she is feeling at the moment. I ponder decisions and make pro/con lists; she works on impulse. In fact, she is very much like my own mother from whom I was so happy to escape when I reached adulthood.

I have often wondered: How in the world did the universe deliver me a child who presented the very same issues that I had struggled so hard to get away from? How many of these personality issues could be influenced by parental instruction? How many were just things she (and we) would have to live with? Why did the consequences we imposed for her misbehavior have no effect? Would this ever get better? When I share this perspective with my workshop group, heads nod in agreement.

Here are some other thoughts I hear from mothers of challenging kids:

"We may never take a family vacation again."

"I worry about my child using drugs and/or alcohol as a way to deal with his/her bad feelings."

"My relationship with my husband and other children is suffering.

I feel so depressed by my inability to make this better."

"The teachers and therapists don't seem to be able to understand or to help in any meaningful way."

"I worry about the judgments of others who think I am a bad parent."

"If I only knew some magic technique, maybe this could be better."

"Did I eat or drink something while pregnant that caused this?"

"What will this mean for my child's future happiness?"

I had all of these thoughts and more. Yikes! How can you feel good about yourself when these thoughts are knocking around inside your noggin?

Having a challenging child supercharged my life. For that reason, I eagerly work with clients facing this same challenge in workshops and individual sessions. As a life coach, I help mothers to confront their dark thoughts about themselves and their children by bringing light to these dark thoughts. By examining other ways of looking at the situation, new possibilities emerge.

My goals during workshops include:

1) Providing a safe place to disclose some of the mothers' bad experiences with their children. The act of saying it out loud can provide a sense of relief, especially when heard by nonjudgmental peers.
2) Determining which part of the problem belongs to the parent and which to the child. As much as we want to make our child's path smoother, we often cannot. However, our behavior and reactions can alter more than we imagine.
3) Taking steps to rebuild self-esteem as a mother and human being.

During a five hour workshop, we can only begin to work on step 3. Individual coaching sessions further the process of healing and moving toward wholeness and joy. Using tools developed by Martha Beck, I work with clients in weekly sessions over a period of months to further resolve these issues. Though work with clients is always fluid, the categories that we cover fall into some general areas:

Whose Journey is it?

Topics to explore:
How much control do we actually have over another person?
How does this change as children move from infancy to adulthood?

Whenever I work with clients, and they have complaints about relationships, I start with the question: Whose business are you in? There are 3 kinds of business: My business, your business, and God's business. *God's business* is all the things no human being can control: the weather, the national economy, your height, etc. *Your business* is all the things that you can control. *My business* is all the things that I can control. The fraction of things that each of us can control is very small, yet very powerful. So powerful that once we harness our thoughts and energy toward changing the things we can change and moving toward our goals, we can transform lives.

Mothers are often conflicted about the distinction between *my business* and *your business* when it comes to their children. The cultural expectation of mothers is that we are responsible for our children's behavior. This can begin with pregnancy worries (I worked in an office cubicle next to two heavy smokers in the days when smoking was allowed at work. Did that cause behavior problems?) and continue through finding the right preschool, advocating for special needs testing, vetting friends and video games, etc. Behavior frustrations often lead to anger and unplanned actions like yelling. How are these harming my child and/or our relationship? If you gave up a professional career to become a stay-at-home mom, there is the pressure of feeling that you need to meet some standard to justify such a decision. If you decide to continue working, there's the guilt associated with the quantity and quality of time spent with the child as well as the child-caretaking decisions. As near as I can tell, no mother in our society escapes this pressure to see the "success" of her children as a measure of her own success, and, therefore, a measure of self-worth.

A fundamental question that I address with these mothers is this: How much control do we actually have over another person? Even if that person is an infant, the answer is surprisingly little. Of course, there are things we do that make a difference. Yet the fundamental personality is laid down by powers out of our control. Figuring out what we can control and what we cannot is key to our own peace of mind.

How does this change as children move from infancy to adulthood? What children need most from us is acceptance and love. To the extent that we can accept children for who they are, we give them the best chance to find their own happiness and success in life's journey. They give us a chance to learn that each individual has his/her own journey; we are only responsible for our journey. Learning that is a gift we can give to our children and to ourselves.

Identifying What Really Matters

Topics to explore:
Who is judging your success as a mother? What is
success as a mother?

Does success in life correlate with success in school?
Do you feel successful?
How does that affect your choices/decisions?

All the mothers I have worked with are wonderful, kind, loving, accomplished women. Not all of them recognize this in themselves as we begin the coaching relationship. Many are very goal-oriented. When working with mothers of challenging children, I often have extensive conversations on ideas of success early in the process. There are at least two dimensions to this discussion: success as a mother, and success for the child. Frequently, the two are tied together. My goal is to untie them and examine them critically.

Early on, I ask clients to define some goals and/or values for their family. These could include items like:

- I want my family to eat dinner together every day.
- I want my family to experience memorable vacations.
- I want my family to be physically active and healthy.
- I want my children to have empathy for others.
- I want the family to go to church together each Sunday.
- I want my children to feel acceptance and love from me.
- I want us to listen empathetically to each other.

Frequently, this process of thinking through family values causes a shift in the client's ideas about success and goals. As the client thinks through what she truly values, she moves to a point where she can reject cultural standards that do not work for her family.

There is often a sense of relief after completion of this step. This relief is primarily because decisions and choices are much easier when we are clear about our values and goals.

After setting goals for the family, discussions of "success" are also easier. It is a lot easier to get to the right train station when you can identify your stop by name. The same is true for success. Too often we blindly follow a cultural norm for our children's success, such as working on Wall Street or going to an Ivy League school. When we define success for our children in terms of what we value (for example, I want my child to find his/her passion), our ideas of success are often broader. This creates more freedom for our children and for ourselves.

Accepting What is

Topics to explore:
What qualities did we hope our children would have?
How do we accept them as they are?
What is "acceptable" behavior? Who defines it?

In the process of setting goals and defining important values, it is critical to be able to accept what is possible to influence and what is not within our control. Like most everyone on this planet, I have a lifetime of suffering caused by complaining about circumstances and wanting things to be different. Giving up the thought that things should be different has led to a deep feeling of liberation and freedom. I seek that freedom for my clients.

Mothers of challenging children usually yearn for things to be different. It can be difficult to sort out acceptable expectations for our children. For example, asking a 5-year old ADD child to sit through a one hour meal in a restaurant may be unreasonable. Expecting him to do it at 10 may be reasonable. Add to that the desire to treat all of our children "equally." My two children were totally different in personality. A reasonable expectation for one was unreasonable for the other. I do not try to "solve" the relationship between the mother and child. If necessary, I suggest books and/or other resources to address that particular issue. Instead, I focus on the client's thoughts about the situation.

One reason why this is so helpful is that our children are often quite intuitive when it comes to reading our thoughts. Even those things we don't say out loud often come across and are assimilated into the child's thinking about his or herself. We fool ourselves into thinking it is safe to think those thoughts if we don't say them out loud. Unfortunately, it just doesn't work out that way. Our thoughts manage to communicate themselves whether said out loud or not. It is better to learn to change our approach toward life by questioning our thoughts about how things should be.

I teach clients how to do this through structured examination of their thoughts. We frequently discover that it is possible to see how changing the thought about the situation can result in quite different behavior on the part of the parent. Different behavior can then influence the relationship with the child and usually makes everyone calmer, happier, and more creative in seeking solutions to the troubling circumstance.

There are various methods of observing and challenging our thoughts. One of the most powerful is The Work by Byron Katie. Her website at www.thework.com provides videos and resources that are extremely powerful when put into practice. A good explanation of this method can also be found in her book, *Loving What Is*. As Stephen Mitchell, Katie's husband and co-author of *A Thousand Names for Joy*, writes in his preface, "Once we deeply question a thought, it loses its power to cause us pain, and eventually it ceases even to arise." I have personally experienced this profound transformation and recommend it to all who experience suffering over various issues.

Desire and Self-Care

Topics to explore:
Did you give up a part of yourself when you had
children? What was it? Can it be reclaimed?
What brought you joy when you were young? Is that
element still a part of your life? Why not?

In our desire to be the perfect mother, we often forget how to nourish ourselves. Self-care goes out the window as indulgent and unnecessary. Sometimes we think it's an issue of time, money, lack of childcare, or an unsupportive spouse. However, there is usually a way to find time for self-care when we realize that it needs to be given some priority.

One of the first things I ask each client to do is to keep a small notebook next to their bed. When they wake in the morning, I ask them to write down, "What I really, really, really want today is...." There is no limit to what you can want either in quantity or quality. Nor is there any expectation that you need to try to accomplish whatever it is. The whole point of the exercise is to help the client focus on her needs and desires. (Proper credit for this exercise goes to Elizabeth Gilbert, author of *Eat Pray Love* who suggested this to listeners on an Oprah show while discussing her book and personal journey.)

Another exercise I ask clients to do is the Sensual Exercise. For mothers who have immersed themselves in the caretaker/provider mode, this can be a surprisingly difficult assignment. Its power is two-fold: to find activities that provide pure pleasure, and to reconnect with their senses and physical body. The exercise can be found in an attachment at the end of this chapter.

I always spend some time exploring the body compass exercise with clients as well. Learning to tune into the innate body wisdom is critical to making good choices in the future. Chapter 2 of *Finding Your Own North Star* by Martha Beck has exercises to help you learn to dial into your body compass.

What is Happiness?

Topics to explore:
How do we define it for ourselves? For our children?
Can everyone be happy?
What would it mean to be happy?
What obstacles stand in the way of your happiness?

Are you in touch with your authentic self? How do you nourish that? How do you make the proper choices to bring more joy and happiness into your life? This is the heart and soul of my individual coaching sessions. Living authentically is key to experiencing more joy and serenity. Although each client sets goals for coaching early in the process, my goal is always to have the client wake up excited each day, knowing that she will have many joyful experiences coming her way. In addition, she will feel confident that she has the tools to handle the challenges that life inevitably throws our way.

Despite the fact that many tears are shed during sessions, my clients report that they look forward to coaching sessions and their homework assignments. My job as a life coach is to challenge their assumptions about themselves and the world around them, to help them define a successful life, and to encourage steps that will lead to a full, joyful life. Almost always, the changes they make in their external world are surprisingly small ones, almost just tweaks to their prior activities. The biggest change is internal: a confidence in identifying their own needs and how to meet them. For my part, I fall in love with each of my clients. It is hard not to, when you see authentic, struggling souls dealing with issues that are as close to their hearts as their children. It is my privilege to help them move toward a brighter future.

Today my daughter and I have a wonderful relationship. It turns out her level of intuition is even higher than mine. We have come to understand and value each other's strengths and weaknesses and to know how to support each other. The challenge that I thought was plaguing my life turned out to be a blessing beyond measure. In leaving behind my old assumptions about the world and how it works, I entered a more joyful place. My life is infinitely richer.

Sensual Exercise Homework Assignment

Give yourself the gift of 15 minutes of pleasure. For the next 7 days, spend a *minimum* of 15 minutes doing something sensual and/or kind to your body. You can do this for yourself at little to no cost – or splurge a little on new products or on a professional. Choose only things that you think will be a pleasure, e.g., if you don't like biking, don't choose that as an activity. Each day should be something different. Try to choose a variety of activities that focus on different senses: smell, taste, sight, touch, hearing. Expand your range of experiences by choosing something fresh and new. Focus on each moment. Concentrate on what the experience is like. Take notes on what felt good, what might have been uncomfortable, what sensations and/or thoughts were generated. Note them on the reporting form and bring them to our session next week.

Some possibilities:

- experience a bubble bath, facial, manicure, pedicure
- get a massage or try reflexology
- wander through the perfume section of a department store or Sephora
- walk somewhere visually scenic, roller-blade, bike
- listen to your favorite music with no distraction and eyes closed
- sit at a playground and watch the young mothers interact with their children

- swing on the playground swingset
- wander through a flower section of a grocery store smelling the flowers
- go to a fabric store and look for textures that you find appealing
- buy a home design magazine and rip out pages that make you feel good
- lay on your back in the sun, close your eyes, and feel your skin warm from the sun's heat
- walk barefoot in the grass
- walk on the beach where the sand meets the water and let the sand squish between your toes
- build a sand-castle with slushy wet sand
- play in the snow
- walk through autumn leaves breathing in the smell and listening to the crunching sound
- make some home-made play dough and play with it
- try some exotic new food and wallow in the new taste sensation
- get some bubble gum and blow bubbles
- get a makeover at a department store counter
- listen to a CD of music you would never choose and observe your reaction to it
- go to the farmer's market and smell all the fresh produce.

Remember that each day should have 15 minutes of concentrated time focused on that experience. Record your reactions immediately afterward.

Sensual Exercise Record

Day 1: What I did: _____

What was the experience like for you? Would you do it again? Why or why not?

_____
_____
_____
_____
_____

Day 2: What I did: _____

What was the experience like for you? Would you do it again? Why or why not?

_____
_____
_____
_____
_____
_____

Day 3: What I did: _____

What was the experience like for you? Would you do it again? Why or why not?

_____
_____
_____
_____
_____
_____

Day 4: What I did: _____

What was the experience like for you? Would you do it again? Why or why not?

_____

_____

_____

_____

_____

_____

Day 5: What I did: _____

What was the experience like for you? Would you do it again? Why or why not?

_____

_____

_____

_____

_____

Day 6: What I did: _____

What was the experience like for you? Would you do it again? Why or why not?

_____

_____

_____

_____

_____

_____

Day 7: What I did: _____

What was the experience like for you? Would you do it again? Why or why not?

_____

_____

_____

_____

_____

_____

ⅭⳄ

I would like to thank my delightful daughter who read this manuscript and gave it a thumbs-up. She has been the spur to achieving my best life; for that I thank the higher powers that exist in this universe.

Holly Berman's calm demeanor, diverse experience, and intuitive connection with others combine with a keen intelligence to empower her coaching practice. Having a good sense of humor enabled Holly to prosper in the profit, not-for-profit, and governmental sectors whether as an employee, elected official, or volunteer. She has a BA in Anthropology from the University of Illinois and an MBA from the University of Chicago. More information on her coaching practice can be found at www.AlethaLife Coaching.com.

ଓ

Living In Gratitude

by Roma Strong Zanders

Gratitude is not only the greatest of virtues,
but the parent of all the others.
– Cicero

Take this moment to think of three things you're grateful for. It's a first step on the way to experiencing a deeper appreciation of your life.

Why live a life of gratitude? Years ago, I wrote down my life's purpose – a sort of personal mission statement. It was simply: "My purpose is to live an intentionally joyful life." One of the fastest ways to joy is to live in gratitude. Joy and gratitude are inner states of being. Most people's first thought is, "Sure, I can be joyful and grateful – and have been – when things are going my way." I believe that regardless of the outer circumstances in our lives (for example, the state of our health, finances, family life, or career), it's possible to live a life filled with gratitude and joy.

Feeling gratitude is also a vital part of the Law of Attraction. If you want to live a life filled with gratitude, remember that the Law of Attraction, at its most basic, states that "like attracts like." Whatever we focus on expands in our life. Why not focus on gratitude and joy? Feeling gratitude is a result of noticing what is available to you right here, right now. Feeling gratitude for the love of family members, the connectedness to friends, the satisfaction of your career, only draws more of that to you. It has to.

*"Gratitude is when memory is stored in the heart
and not the mind."*
– Lionel Hampton

When you found the three things you're grateful for, where did they come from? Did they come from the head or the heart? When I started intentionally noticing gratitude, I found that I was approaching it as a mental exercise. "Okay, before I go to bed, I need to write down what I am grateful for today. Let's see... I'm grateful for my nieces, I'm grateful for the interesting book I'm reading, and I'm grateful that I live so close to excellent hiking trails. Done." It's not that I didn't *mean* it, or that I wasn't genuinely grateful for these things. It's just that it rarely went beyond a mental exercise – my thoughts and my reasonable answers.

Gradually, I became aware that I was noticing gratitude from within. Now, at the end of the day, I ask myself what I was grateful for throughout the day, and instead of mentally scanning the day, I wait. I notice what arises from somewhere inside of me, somewhere other than my head. My heart. And the list becomes more and more refined. For some, that may be a subtle difference. For me, it was a huge shift. Having hot water, seeing my niece Natalie reach for my husband's hand when we walk, my niece Meridia's beautiful silky hair, hearing birds sing a song just for me, the single gardenia that bloomed outside overnight, being able to breathe deeply. These things enriched my day, and I was grateful for them. And I was grateful for slowing down enough to notice them.

Notice three things you're grateful for. Come from the heart and not the head. Ask yourself, "What am I grateful for in this moment?" Take a deep breath, and wait to see what emerges from the heart.

Are the three things you're grateful for tangible or intangible?

Now, add three more things you're grateful for so that you have three tangible things and three intangible things.

Gratitude can be multi-faceted – if you tend to weight your gratitude more on intangibles, realize that it's okay to be grateful for tangibles. If you tend to be grateful for tangibles, understand that some of the best things in life are intangibles.

For me, in this moment, they are: the sweater that's keeping me warm, my computer that keeps me in touch with everyone, and my husband, who knows how to do all sorts of mechanical things around the house (which he's doing right now). I'm also grateful for the long, restful sleep I had last night, the flexibility of my schedule today, and for living close to my sister and her family.

Can you find more?

> *He is a wise man who does not grieve for the*
> *things which he has not,*
> *but rejoices for those which he has.*
> *– Epictetus*

At first, when my clients are motivated to cultivate gratitude in their lives and to start becoming aware of the abundance all around them – and either aren't used to or are uncomfortable with doing this – I have them use one or more of the following simple techniques:

- *Find a "gratitude partner."* My sister, Caroline, and I do this. We share gratitude experiences. For example, I recently called Caroline to tell her about "being blessed." My husband I were at a drive-through coffee shack, and when the woman handed us our drinks (and freshly-made donuts) she said that the gentleman ahead of us paid for our order and handed us a card that said "You've just been blessed by a member of Heritage Baptist Fellowship." We were so grateful for that small (big, with the donuts!), spontaneous act of kindness. Later that day, I called my sister to share the story and tell her that that was on top of my gratitude list for the day. She then shared with me where she had noticed gratitude and appreciation for that day. We did this for several weeks, knowing that we had to tell one another at least one thing we were grateful for each evening, which helped us to be aware and to be present – during the day.

- *Keep a list throughout the day.* I suggest clients keep a pad of paper on their desk, or wherever it's handy and visible, to be able to write down spontaneous thoughts and feelings of gratitude. When they are getting into the habit of noticing and cultivating gratitude, it helps to keep a running list. It's easier than doing it only at night and having to think back throughout the day, when the little things that they felt thankful for elude them. One client found that when she kept a list on her desk, she found several things she was grateful for: a pen that was given as a gift and that she loves to use, receiving funny e-mails to break up the work day, being able to take an extra fifteen minutes for lunch, a client who unexpectedly called and told her how much he liked the product she sold him. She realized that small things like this might not have made her list at the end of the day.

- *Have gratitude for breakfast.* While you're having breakfast, or while you're commuting to work, find three things you're grateful for. Do it first thing in the morning, when you're (hopefully) rested and your mind isn't so active with your daily to-do list. Now I like making a gratitude list at the beginning of the day more than I do at the end of the day, for just that reason. Remember, you don't have to make it too serious. Ask yourself what you're grateful for, and then wait a few moments. See what comes up. It could be that you're grateful for things as simple as a hot shower, that you woke up on time, that it's a sunny day, that you unloaded the dishwasher the night before and don't have to do it this morning (that's mine). Maybe you're grateful for simply waking up!

If noticing gratitude is new for you, commit to finding a gratitude partner, keeping a list throughout the day, and/or having gratitude for breakfast consistently for two weeks.

There is a calmness to a life lived in gratitude, a quiet joy.
– Ralph H. Blum

Much of what you're grateful for may be right in front of you or all around you. You may even be taking it for granted. When I asked a client what she was grateful for, she was quiet for quite some time. After awhile, I asked if she was grateful for her children's health, her beautiful home, the flexibility of her part-time job. "Well, yeah, there are *those* things," she said, "but that's just a given. Of course I'm grateful for them. But I'm trying to think of other things, things that aren't so obvious."

I call that the *macro* and the *micro* of gratitude. Yes, there are the *big* things that I feel grateful for and don't often acknowledge – my home, my dependable car, my loving spouse, my health, my benefits at work. And don't we often take them for granted, until we hear of someone who has lost a home, a spouse, a job?

Make a macro gratitude list. Then read through your list and feel – not just think – about how you're grateful for these things in your life.

My macro list includes our comfortable new home, our gas-efficient hybrid car, living a few miles from my sister and her family, my nearly-inexhaustible energy level, my view of the mountains, living in the country near a small town, my healthy body, and my fabulous husband.

Now make a micro gratitude list. Then read through your list and feel – not just think – about how you're grateful for these things in your life.

My micro list includes not having to set an alarm in the morning, my daily cup of Kona coffee, having TiVo, my personalized stationery, and being able to video chat with all my family members.

"When you are grateful, fear disappears
and abundance appears."
– Anthony Robbins

Recently a client said to me, "When I'm in a place of gratitude, I can't be in a place of worry." It's true – you can't be in a place of worry, sadness, fear, doubt, anger, or loneliness when you're in a place of gratitude, when you are thankful for the things that bring you happiness, contentment, and joy.

Notice if this is true for you: the next time you are worried, sad, or fearful, think of what brings you a feeling of gratitude, and notice whether or not you can hold both at the same time.

"At times our own light goes out and is rekindled by a spark from another person. Each of us has cause to think with deep gratitude of those who have lighted the flame within us."
– Albert Schweitzer

What about being grateful for the challenging areas of your life? Losing a job, having a debilitating illness, getting audited by the IRS, having unexpected home repairs, having a parent slip into dementia? Do you experience gratitude for these situations? Are you thankful for the situations you label "bad"?

In the last several months I have had bouts of frustration and anger at our country's financial situation – at corporate managers and leaders, at specific cabinet members and government officials, at radio talk show hosts who spew anger and never seem to offer solutions. Even at fellow citizens who I thought had contributed to the mess. One day I wrote down all my judgments about the financial situation. What I found most stressful was the thought, "We, as Americans, are not going to learn anything from this financial crisis." Then, I did The Work. The Work of Byron Katie is an amazingly simple, yet profound process of asking four questions and finding turnarounds to the original stressful thought. Simply put, it's a way to inner peace – a way to see reality for what it is, not what I *want* it to be. I did The Work on my stressful thoughts around our country's financial situation and what I perceived as our lack of ethical standards, our greedy corporate leaders, our in-it-for-themselves government officials, the mean-spirited and unproductive radio and TV commentators. I came to a place of peace after questioning my thoughts. A place of more balanced understanding. And then I asked myself, "What is the gift in this situation?" After spending quite a bit of time thinking about it, I came to a place of gratitude. *Genuine* gratitude.

What was I grateful for? I found that I was thankful that this crisis occurred as we were electing a new president (regardless of who won). I found where we, as a country, have changed or altered course in the past when we've needed to. I also felt that, as painful as this recession may be to many Americans, it presents an opportunity to change the way we do business in this country – how we choose to compensate our top executives, what regulations we put in place to protect the investing public, and how we can operate our businesses ethically. These are the thoughts that felt true to me and what I felt gratitude for – they may or may not be true for you.

In my experience, it has been the most challenging times in my life that have led me to question my stressful thoughts, which has brought me to a profound sense of gratitude. It's a whole different degree of feeling gratitude – an advanced level of gratitude. The next level. Phase II.

There was a time when I was very stressed out about a person close to me. You name it, I felt it about this person. I was constantly annoyed and frustrated, and I was full of critical thoughts: they were rude, subjective in their opinions, sarcastic, ungrateful, tiresome, too talkative, and just plain stupid. Even saying "there was a time" isn't the whole story. I felt this way about this person for more than two decades. These thoughts weren't with me all the time, but they would come-and-go as we interacted with one another, and I felt the feelings strongly. Not only that, I was sure that I was correct in my opinions – didn't everyone feel this way about this person? I'd seek out people who shared my thoughts, and add to my stress level the unpleasant feeling – and knowledge – of being a gossip, being unkind, and definitely not treating someone how I wanted to be treated.

Then I did The Work. Again and again I'd identify a stressful thought about this person and use The Work's four questions and turnarounds. Until finally, one day, I understood deeply – at a feeling level, not just a knowing level – that this person was a complete mirror of me. I saw in this person what I wasn't willing to see in myself. Until that moment. And that's when I felt a deep sense of gratitude toward this person and discovered how thankful I am that they're in my life. I noticed other wonderful qualities they possess that I had been unwilling to acknowledge. I was able to find several answers to "What is the gift in this situation?" and "What gift does this person hold for me?"

Think about a recent situation that was challenging or difficult. As you think about the situation, can you answer the question, "What is the gift in this situation?" or "What am I grateful for in this situation?"

*"Feeling gratitude and not expressing it is like
wrapping a present and not giving it."*
– William Arthur Ward

Is it enough to only *notice* what you're grateful for? For me, it's just the beginning. And the noticing, the awareness, is only the first step. Expressing it is the next step. How do you express your gratitude? In words? In deeds? In writing?

You can express your gratitude in a variety of ways: keeping a gratitude journal, writing a thank you note, telling someone you're grateful for something they've done for you or something they've given to you, doing something special for someone you're grateful for. Here are three ways I've expressed gratitude recently: I said "thank you" to the guy who picks up my recycling (I had lots of it and he had to do some serious loading), I gave my husband a foot rub after a long day of working around the house, and I wrote a letter to a salesperson who recently helped me with a time-consuming order.

Intentionally express your gratitude three times today.

*If you concentrate on finding whatever is
good in every situation,
you will discover that your life will suddenly
be filled with gratitude,
a feeling that nurtures the soul.
– Rabbi Harold Kushner*

Gratitude is a mindful choice, an intentional choice. I believe it's a skill you can develop and perfect, until one day it's simply a part of who you are and not what you do.

Here are some ideas on how to intentionally bring more gratitude into your life:

- *Keep a daily gratitude journal where you write out or simply list what you're grateful for.* You decide how many items to list each day – one may feel right in the beginning, or three may be a good number to try for. Or, you may not want to make it that structured. One day there may be a lot of things on your list; other days there may only be a few. One reason I like to have a number as a goal is that it stretches me to look a little deeper, to go further than I may normally have done. Plus, I think more gratitude is always better. My favorite gratitude journal is the 5-Year Journal which lets me see what I was grateful for on any particular day the previous one, two, three, or four years.

- *Create a gratitude jar or bowl.* I have colorful strips of paper in my desk to write on when I'm overcome with a feeling of gratitude. I fill out a strip of paper, roll it up, and put it in a bowl in my office. What I love about my gratitude bowl is that it's beautiful to look at, and it's a visual reminder of all the things I have to be grateful for. Whereas my gratitude journal is tucked away on the bookshelf, my gratitude bowl is something that I look at many times each day (and it always makes me smile). Plus, it's a great conversation piece for people who see it and ask what all those colorful strips of paper curled up in the bowl are for.

- *Keep a family gratitude album or journal.* Place a journal, album, or simply a notebook in a place where each family member can contribute to it regularly.

This is a way to get everyone involved, and help your kids to cultivate an attitude of gratitude with you. Encourage everyone to be creative – use words, pictures, quotes, different colored pens, and different handwriting to make it fun to use and fun to look at.

- *Thank one person every day for something.* When you feel genuinely grateful to someone, take the time to thank them. This can be in person, on the phone, over the computer, or my favorite – write it in a card or letter. I agree with W. A. Ward when he says that not expressing gratitude is like wrapping a gift and not giving it. It doesn't matter to me how my gratitude is accepted, whether it's with appreciation or indifference. I'm aware that I do this because it makes *me* feel good.

- *Create a ritual around gratitude.* I have a friend who has two small bowls – one initially filled with beautiful, smooth, small natural rocks she's found while walking or hiking, and the other one is empty. Each time she thinks of someone or something she's grateful for, she transfers a rock from one bowl to the other. I love the visual and tactile nature of this ritual. When I've done this, I feel gratitude for the perfectly formed rocks, the trips I've taken to find them, and the person or situation that made me transfer a rock in the first place!

- *Say grace at every meal.* I had stopped doing this years ago because saying a rote prayer before each meal felt like a hollow ritual to me. Gradually, however, I started finding my own way to express gratitude at each meal. Usually it's just pausing to feel the gratitude for all the unknown people who helped put the variety of food on my plate, and for my good fortune that I could afford such healthy food. Now, when my husband and I are together, or my sister and her family are over for a meal, before we eat we take the time to say thank you for the food and each of us says something we were grateful for that day. When I hear what the others are grateful for, I pause to see if I can find a sense of gratitude for that same thing myself. They help me find places of gratitude with people and situations that I hadn't thought of before.

Think of the ways you'd like to bring more gratitude into your life.

Silent gratitude isn't much use to anyone.
– G.B. Stern

Why live in gratitude? Of course, there's the research that says it makes you healthier, and it engages the law of attraction in a positive way – bringing more and more gratitude and joy to you. But it simply comes down to bringing us closer to our true nature – love. Love for myself, love for others, love for what's right here, right now.

To all those reading these words, I wish for you a life of joy and a life lived

In Gratitude,

Roma

ᥴ

I'm grateful for the wonderful, supportive people in my life: my sisters, Chryl and Caroline; the world's best parents, Daryl & Bette Strong; the most interesting friends, Sandra and Gael; and my all-time favorite person, my husband, Paul – having you in my life is a constant joy. And thank you, Dad, for teaching – and showing – the four of us kids that "success is doing what you love to do."

Roma Strong Zanders has been coaching for years. She brings a wide range of experience to her clients – she's owned a business, worked for large and small businesses, enjoyed years as a homemaker, and finds time to read, hike, travel, help out with her nieces, and volunteer as a court mediator. She's grateful for many things, including living in the Pacific Northwest with her husband of 22 years. You can learn more about Roma at http://www.coachroma.com.

ଔ

Embracing Change

Align Your Personal Strengths with Your True Purpose

by Ned Rios

Defining Change

Do you want to initiate change in your life but you're unsure how? Do you want to improve a situation, a relationship, a career, a certain part of your life or your emotions? What is change and how do you define it? Change can be defined as moving from one state to another; creating something different; causing transformation. I wrote this chapter on embracing change for those craving to move into a new career, or looking to find their true purpose.

I want to teach you a process that will help you align your purpose in life with your passion. When we align our strengths with what gives us natural energy, we unveil our passion and purpose. Sometimes, we know what we want to do in life and sometimes we become crippled with fear. Fear of not knowing what we want and fear of change. That fear can stop our ability to grow and achieve goals. However, once you have a good understanding of why you want to change, and identify the desire to birth your true purpose, then you begin to unfold into a path meant for you.

Planned change is the catalyst to achieve self-growth and progress. Bringing new ideas and new developments can lead to a fulfilling personal life or career. Change can be proactive and manageable. Change can also be reactionary and inevitable. We face change daily because it is the evolution of life. The one thing we know for sure about change is that it is everywhere, evolving all around us, all of the time. We have choices: we can embrace change or resist it.

Empower Yourself

When we empower ourselves in situations that we can control, we can start changing our life. Gandhi said it best, "Be the change you want to see in the world." Change starts with us. Many times our own decisions drive the results we get in life. If your decisions are made full of fear and doubt, the results are untrue to what we truly want. As Tony Robbins said, "More than anything else I believe it's our decisions, not the conditions of our lives, that determine our destiny." We, as human beings, get in our own way of having what we want.

When I sit with my clients, I see what kind of suffering they give themselves when they don't take risks in their lives because of fear – fear that is driven by their own thoughts. They are afraid of the uncertainty and of the unsettling feelings that they could face. But we cannot grow without risk – and the challenges we face are here to teach us something. Self growth is human nature, much like breathing. So you can imagine what we could do to ourselves when we don't take the leap we truly desire.

Why are we so scared of change? Could it be that when we do not know where a plan may take us, it causes uncertainty? Although change can bring new opportunities and improvements in our lives, it also can add uncertainty and doubt. Once we get adjusted to a certain state in our life, we feel comfortable and don't want to seek change anymore. The problem is that we start compromising our dreams based on the notion that not changing brings stability and security to our lives. Since we don't want to compromise our security, we are robbed from achieving our true desire. Sometimes we could be scared because change can be like walking in fog, we can't see the destination – but we can make the whole trip one step at a time.

Once you accept that you want change, allow yourself to embrace the feeling of wanting change, rather than introducing worry, fear, or stress. When we begin to experience worry, fear, and stress, then we are creating resistance to change in some way. When our negative thoughts/limiting beliefs get in the way of our true desires then we know that there may be some resistance. Let your heart manage your life and use your mind as a tool to reach the goals you want.

Is it really fear that we feel or our thoughts dictating our life? I think it could be a combination of both. When I was at my last position I remember thinking that I didn't want to be a quitter if I resigned. That thought was causing me to feel distressed and then created the action of doing nothing. The result of the thought was that I would stop dead in my tracks and force myself to stay in a place that I felt was toxic and unhealthy. So I am here to say that life does happen after realizing that your own thoughts can hold you captive to a life you don't really want. We all have thoughts that could turn into beliefs and those become limiting because they stop us from doing what we really want to do. (Inspired by The Work of Byron Katie)

Obstacles: Where do the beliefs come from?

Limiting Beliefs are thoughts that hold you back from getting what you want. There are three basic types of limiting beliefs: 1) Our Own Beliefs, 2) Social Beliefs, and 3) Learned Beliefs.

As we grow and have different experiences in life, we create our own rules and expectations that we place on ourselves. They could be based on a bad situation you experienced, leading you to create a thought that leads to a limiting belief.

Social beliefs are the ones that come from our society, work, friends, and family. We all walk around in this world believing and reinforcing each other's limiting beliefs sometimes. I call it the capsule syndrome, because once we are encapsulated in each other's beliefs, we stop seeing life outside the capsule. Once you begin reinforcing each other's limiting beliefs then you are no longer living your own life nor being open minded. Suffering from your own thoughts is painful but worst of all is having other people reinforce the limiting beliefs.

Learned beliefs are sometimes unconscious. These are the beliefs that you learned as a child from your parents and people close to you. Have you ever said or done something to a friend or spouse that reminded you of what your parents would say? You probably didn't even like that behavior when you grew up. It all happens unconsciously and the good news is you can change it.

So how can we make sure the people around us are good for us? Throughout this process, remember you must always surround yourself with people who will support your true desires. Find like-minded friends that are honest and encourage you. The most important thing to remember is that it all starts with us – in our own belief system first. Do you believe in your dream? Do you believe you can find your purpose and make it happen?

Try asking yourself these questions:

What kind of change do I yearn for?
What kind of work would allow me to follow my dream?
What talent or strength do I have that I enjoy and would love to capitalize on?

The most important thing to remember is you deserve to do what you love. The answers to these questions will hopefully spark interest and give you personal direction.

Defining your Change

Discovery

This process isn't just about choosing a career, job, or passion. This is about choosing your best lifestyle. A life that gives you meaning and a quality of life that fits you. To everyone, this is defined differently. To get the most from this chapter, be 100% true to yourself and open to all possibilities. When I went through this process, I had just gotten married. My husband and I had big careers and we were both traveling extensively. Most importantly, I was not fulfilled at my job, since I had taken it based on what I thought was the "next logical step" in my career. I had to ask myself what kind of lifestyle I wanted, what type of career I yearned for, and what type of relationship I wanted. The thought of changing was scary, and at the same time liberating. We both learned that the option to be liberated had more benefits than the risk of staying in the same situation.

Inner child

Let's find your yearning. If you are having trouble identifying things that you love to do, I say go to your inner child. As a child we have the freedom to dream without restrictions. We do not concern ourselves with bills, work, or children. Whether you are trying to lose weight or find a new career, remember the activities you enjoyed as a child. Did you make jewelry, sew, ride a bike, dress up, play tennis, or play a musical instrument? Did you enjoy reading or writing? Think of any activity that you considered fun and remember how that made you feel. Do you still feel the same now? When you are enjoying yourself, it allows you to shift energy into a more positive flow. Everyone has one activity they found easy and fun. When you were a child, you tended to just have fun and never concern yourself with your own thoughts. When you participate in activities that are effortless and fun, it is inspiring and brings new ideas. Sometimes hobbies turn into careers and sometimes they just stay as hobbies, yet they still fulfill you. This process is not just about figuring out what you want, it is also about incorporating joy in your life and creating balance and wellness. So when you make that connection with your inner child, you will be amazed at the results and the feelings you begin to experience. (Inspired from Martha Beck's work.)

Things I know for sure that come easy to me

We each have something that comes natural to us, but the key is that it must also feel good and give you strength. You could be an accountant and numbers might come naturally to you. But if every time you do this activity it depletes your energy, then you are not being true to yourself and you may not be in the career best suited for you.

Exercise: Take out a white piece of paper and a crayon or marker. I find that a crayon is fun and links you with your inner child. Write down all activities that are easy for you. Please include basic things like:

- Communicating with people
- Playing guitar
- Working with Excel spreadsheets

Sometimes what other people rely on you for or ask you to do for them, over and over, will be a good indicator of these activities. However, that doesn't mean that will be your career – it just means you are identifying what comes easy for you. Identifying what comes naturally for you is the first step. If it also gives you energy, feels effortless, and, most importantly, feels good – then you may be on to something for yourself.

Next step, rank activities from 1 to 5, giving 5 to those activities that give you positive energy and strength. Give 1 to activities that give you the least interest or completely deplete your energy.

Natural talent that feels good + activity that gives you strength = doing what you love   (true purpose).

Figuring out where you are

Do you like your job but not the environment?   Yes/no
Do you completely dislike what you do everyday?   Yes/no
Does your job fulfill you but you dislike your
boss?   Yes/no
Do you want to spend more time with family?   Yes/no
Do you want to improve quality of life?   Yes/no
Do you want your own business?   Yes/no
Do you have a passion and want to use it?   Yes/no
Do you need to find your passion?   Yes/no
Are you completely and utterly unfulfilled?   Yes/no

If none of the above apply to you then write in your reason for "career or life not working:"_____

_____

If you answered yes to just one, you may need an element of change. Change doesn't have to be big or small but it must be meaningful to you.

Once you have answered these questions you now have a starting point as we begin the additional exercises.

TIP: Still unsure if you need change?
Here are 3 basic indicators to consider some type of change:

1) You always feel the grass is greener.
2) You wake up and say "Is this all there is to life?"
3) Your happiness is contingent upon something else (I will be happy when my kids are off to school, I will be happy when I have my dream house, I will be happy when I have my dream job, etc).

What is your change agent?

Why do you really want this change? That is the most important question to ask yourself. Knowing why you want to change will give you more strength to reach the career or passion you desire.

What is a change agent? I would define a change agent as something that is causing you distress, but in a healthy way. It is something that creates a yearning to change, fueled by passion and never looking to the past mistakes to define your future. It is a catalyst for self-motivation. A change agent propels you in the right direction and identifies your true hunger for something else.

I saw my personal change agent when I realized my life looked good on paper but didn't feel good in my heart. I was not being honest with myself. Sometimes the turbulence of life leads us to take our boat on a different path and navigate ourselves in a different direction. I arrived at my change agent because I did not feel good in my heart about my career.

What is your change agent?

Below, write what you consider is your main change agent. Some examples are:

- Feeling depleted or drained
- Yearning for your own business
- Emotionally and physically tired
- Burned out
- Compromising family over work
- Improving your quality of life

My change agent is _____

_____

Now since you have identified your change agent, you can move along to what I feel is the most important part of choosing a new career or passion. It is deciding on what type of lifestyle you prefer. Work and lifestyle go hand in hand. You can't have a great career if it disagrees with your lifestyle. Many times we choose careers that do not fit our lives. So think about what type of lifestyle you want first and foremost. Do you want to work at home? Do you only want to work in the mornings? Do you want to work part-time and be home for your kids? So when I was headed in the wrong direction for a career, I had to really think about the lifestyle I wanted. Traveling extensively was not part of it.

Below, think about and write 3 benefits you would gain from the lifestyle you want to achieve. Be specific:

The lifestyle I choose will allow me to _____,
_____, _____.

Becoming fearless

I believe everything we do in life needs courage. As Maya Angelou said so graciously, "Courage is the most important of all the virtues, because without courage you can't practice any other virtue consistently." Courage propels you into taking action. Without courage, the plan never becomes a reality. Here is an exercise to help you find your courage:

Exercise:

Go back to a place in your life where you felt most confident. You may have many or only one. Choose one that best fits and write it down below. (This can pertain to any aspect of your life.)

I feel most confident when I _____
_____

I feel most empowered in my life when _____
_____

I believe in myself 100% when I _____
_____

Now fill out the rest of the exercise below. Be totally honest with yourself and completely truthful. The power of this exercise comes from allowing yourself to go into a feeling of being fearless and uninhibited.

*I know that I want*_____
_____

I know that I want _____
_____

*I know that I want*_____
_____

When I did this exercise myself I didn't think much about it until a few months later. Then I realized that everything I wrote down was already coming true. 1) Resign from current job. 2) Become a life coach. 3) Spend more time with my husband.

Removing Limiting Beliefs

I believe that when there is an element of not feeling good or worthy enough, we start believing we cannot have what we want. For example, when you say things like: "I can't find a good paying job doing what I love," or "I will never find a loving spouse," or "I will never be able to live my passion," those thoughts paralyze you and prohibit you from moving forward. We must closely identify the pattern of thoughts that you may have created. Sometimes we are aware of these thoughts, other times we are so used to our internal chatter that we really do not know how to change it. Always begin this process by just becoming aware of your thinking. One way you can do this is by listening to yourself and recognizing the power of your own words and how they affect you. Instead of using words like "I should" or "I can't," try words like "I want to" or "I choose to." This makes a big difference because of the feeling and energy shift it creates. Let me give you some examples.

I once had a client that was yearning for his own business. Each time we would begin coaching he would say, "I won't be able to have my own business." Using questions inspired by Byron Katie, I would ask him how he feels when he thinks that thought and he said "I feel inadequate." I then asked what type of action he takes towards his business when he thinks that thought, and he replied "I do nothing." When you are trying to initiate a new endeavor in your life, it is important to keep track of your thought patterns, because your thoughts create your feelings and your feelings create your actions. His negative thought alignment did not match his true desires of wanting a business.

Another client was turning 40 and he really wanted to find a job that he would love and enjoy. He was clever and smart and knew exactly what he wanted to do but one thought holding him back was: "Since I graduated from college it has been so hard for me to find a good job," and then I realized that he had been carrying around that limiting belief for 20+ years. He truly believed that it was hard for him. Then he mentioned how that thought made him feel frustrated which stopped him from searching for a job.

I ask that you really begin identifying thoughts and limiting beliefs that have inevitably become part of your everyday language by using the model below. Sometimes you already know what the thoughts are and you can start there; sometimes you must really stop and pay attention to your thinking. Just becoming aware of your thinking is a great accomplishment because it shifts your consciousness and perspective.

If you look at the model below you can take a feeling or a thought and insert it. That allows you to see how that specific thought or emotion is affecting you and possibly holding you back. Your attitudes, thoughts and beliefs affect your ultimate wellness. Why is that important? Because in order for us to make decisions we need to be in an emotionally well place. By using the Thoughts Feelings Actions model (see figure on next page) you can insert a feeling or a thought, which ever one you can identify first, to determine which thoughts are not good for you. The goal is to replace a harmful thought with a better feeling thought that you believe (an adaptation of Self Coaching 101 and inspired by the work of Brooke Castillo.)

Sometimes we know what we are feeling and we may not know the thought causing the feeling. Example: sometimes we know we are sad but we do not know what thought is causing the sadness, creating minimum action. If you jot down notes or journal, you can identify the specific thought and place it in the model. My personal example: I don't want to be a quitter (thought)→gave me the feeling of being defeated →result stayed in a job unhealthy for me.

Besides using the model below you can also journal your thoughts. It is helpful to see what you are thinking through writing. You can journal when you are mad, sad, angry, happy etc. You will be amazed at the pattern of your thinking when you see it on paper.

Thoughts-Feelings-Actions Model

Power of believing in yourself

The power of believing in yourself is the confirmation of knowing you are good enough

The power of believing in yourself is the confirmation that you are deserving

The power of believing in yourself is so strong because no matter who is around

No one can ever take it away from you because it's yours

The power of believing in yourself is the power to validate who you are

The power of believing in yourself is trusting

The power of believing in yourself feels like victory in your heart

The power of believing in yourself feels safe

The power of believing in yourself is true love

The power of believing in yourself is the energy of who you are

The power of believing in yourself brings ultimate joy
The power of believing in yourself feels like freedom
The power of believing in yourself is ultimate passion
The power of believing in yourself is Inner spirit
The power of believing in yourself is in each one of us and sometimes lost
The power to believe in ourselves is always 100% true for us
The power to believe in ourselves is always being grateful for the outcome even if it's not what you were hoping for.
The power of believing in yourself always feels empowering
The power of believing in yourself feels good in our hearts

4 Steps to the power of believing in yourself

1. Love yourself and know that you are always good enough.
2. Write down affirmations that feel good to you.
3. Believe the affirmations.
4. Create the discipline to practice your positive affirmations in front of a mirror because it is a small step to change.

How can you apply the power of believing within you?

Motivation and 3 ways to get started

What is the quality of your motivation? How healthy is your motivation? Are you motivated to prove your thoughts wrong? Are you motivated based on what everyone else wants for you?

I want to teach you how to be motivated in a healthy way.

Motivation is the set of reasons that empower one's ability to engage in a particular behavior. Find out the key reasons that motivate you. Motivation comes from an internal natural state of being joyful. You could start by making a list of activities that you enjoy. Add a new column, and write the reason(s) for doing each activity. Then in a third column, write an immediate action you can take to start engaging in this behavior. The idea is to minimize activities of pain and maximize activities of pleasure.

Speaking engagement → I want to inspire people, empower them → start doing free seminars at local libraries or schools.

Taking photos → spend time outside, connect with nature → spend next Saturday at a local park.

Sometimes certain activities are not the most fun, but they are still required to fulfill activities that you love. For example, if you are photographer, your passion might lie in the art of taking photos. But in order to support that passion, you need to advertise, talk to potential clients, invoice them and collect payment. You might not be fond of these activities and some might stress you out. You might need to empower yourself to change your approach. Delegate some activities and ask for help so you can focus on your strengths. Do some of them in a fun environment. See the opportunity, rather than the limitations.

If all the activities you participate in deplete your natural energy, then it is time to toss them out. When I worked at a software company in sales, I soon realized the work I was doing was completely depleting me. I am an extremely extroverted person and I get my energy from people and the outdoors. Instead, I was in a cube in a very quiet environment, selling something I didn't enjoy.

Motivation makes change easier. For example, I am motivated by feeling strong and feeling in control. Since I know that, it empowers me to eat well and take care of myself.

I participate in activities such as yoga and weight training while eating foods that give me energy. Below I have put together three ways that will help shift your consciousness, your perspective, and your energy.

1) **Morning Fuel** – When you are trying to create change, the first 10 minutes of your day are the most important because it makes you feel in control of your life and sets the tone for the day.

Imagine starting your day doing something you love. How do you think the rest of the day will unfold? How could you spend the first 10 minutes of your day?

One thing you do that makes you feel in control of your life and feels good:

_____

Examples: Spend time with kids, run, read a chapter from a book, listen to music, sing, etc.

The first ten minutes of my day I will_____ because it makes me feel _____.

Make a plan by taking small steps that work for you.

2) **Be Grateful** – Gratitude and appreciation have an incredible ability to shift energy.

When you are feeling negative and feeling bad about everything, I always recommend beginning a gratitude journal. Each day you write 1-3 things you are grateful for in the journal. The key is not to repeat any of them and continue for at least 30-60 days. You will begin to experience a natural shift in energy that will be a catalyst for positive change.

3) **Body, Mind and Soul Shifting** – Take a different approach.

Change something – change your furniture, your clothes, rearrange shelves in the house, move photos or paintings, reorganize your work space. Whatever you do, take a small approach by creating a small change in your environment. The importance of this is to give you a renewed energy and create new energy flow. Example: You can create or find a shelf in your house to place items that reflect who you are and what you love. That way, you have a place that you can go to for inspiration. Some clients have photos, shells, diplomas, awards, art, etc. Use any objects that are meaningful to you. Inspiration is a key component that allows a natural flow of joy.

3 Quick Tips to Combat Daily Negative Thoughts

Here are 3 ways to recognize negative thoughts that might appear in your daily life.

1. **Journal** – Keep a journal of your thoughts. It is helpful not to judge your thoughts and just focus on getting it on paper. This helps you identify the inner chatter you may be having with yourself: name calling, negative thoughts etc. This will allow you time to regroup and realign your

thoughts by looking at them objectively. (See Thought, Feeling, Action model.)

2. **Meditate** – Allow yourself breathing space in your head by abandoning thoughts in your mind. Try doing an activity or meditation that helps you relax. For example, try a couple of minutes of quiet time, a walk in the park, stretching or relaxing in a way that helps you feel refreshed.

3. **Affirmations** – Repeat the mantras (new thoughts) that you really believe, like "I am beginning to become healthy," "I am learning to stay calm," and "I am following my heart and pursuing my dreams." Your positive thoughts will create positive feelings which will turn into inspired actions.

In Summary

Our mind is powerful. We are raised to believe that it is the only tool to make things happen in our lives. But it is in your heart that you truly have the answers. Use your heart as a guide, because it is never wrong. When we decide to disconnect our mind from our body and heart, we become powerless human beings, far more than we realize.

If you are living solely in your thinking, then you are disregarding your heart. You will then detach from who you really are. It is important to unite your heart, mind, and body. Your heart knows your true desires; your mind is the tool to get you there.

Here are some things to keep in mind when embracing change and taking the leap:

1) Risk what feels good to you and take small steps. Small steps become big steps later. Take the time to

discover what you really want and use the tools to guide you.

2) The power of believing in yourself and your personal dream is all that matters. Things will not happen overnight but you will begin to see your vision unfolding.

3) Remember when you face obstacles and you want to give up: Ask yourself what would happen if you never pursued what you truly wanted.

As human beings, we can become comfortable with the life we have, even though it is not the life we want. We might falter in living for things that do not matter, but it is the power of purpose in life that keeps your body well, your mind cleansed, and your heart full of love and happiness. Many times we might feel that taking a risk will bring something worse than what is really out there. Sometimes we wait for tragedy, crisis, or loss to make a change because it is then that the ego is completely dissolved and we make decisions with our heart. I ask instead that you make a change that you really want because you hunger for it like food and desire it like love. For it is not only the dream that we want in life, but the feeling of knowing that we are moving closer to it. This is my definition of embracing change: to identify what you truly want and create the courage and power to make it happen.

We are all born with a purpose but we all have different strengths. I encourage you to find the strength that leads you to a fulfilling life doing what you love. If you feel a void or emptiness in your career, begin now. It is never too late to find what you are truly meant to do in this life.

For me, embracing change meant becoming a life coach. It is the most natural thing I know how to do. It is my gift that I want to share and my passion that makes me feel alive and awakened to who I am.

 C3

To my amazing husband for all of the love and support; to my family for always believing in me. Gratitude and thanks for my clients that allow me to do the work that I love. Thanks to my personal friends and coaches for all the teachings and support. With great thanks to Martha Beck for allowing me to share my light.

Ned Rios is a Certified Life Coach specializing in Change to finding meaningful careers through wellness. She teaches you a process that helps individuals peel back layers of limiting beliefs, set goals, and create inspired actions. She provides one on one coaching, workshops, and speaking engagements. Ned holds a Bachelor of Business Administration in Marketing and a major in Psychology. Prior to coaching, she was a Sales and Marketing professional for 15 years in various positions including career development, account management, and marketing. Ned resides in Houston, Texas with her husband Rey. http://www.tranquilityalive.com

Please see bibliography on p. 257.

 CB

What Are You Really Hungry For?

The Truth About Losing Weight and Keeping it off for Good

by Erin Postle, M.Ed.

"Tell your fat girlfriend to lose weight!" I'll never forget those cutting, horrible words as they were hurled towards me from a passing car full of teenagers. My stomach flopped and my eyes stung with tears as I tried to hide the hurt from this terrible public shaming. After I hung my head and let out a nervous chuckle, I continued walking with my brother towards the nightclub. Of course he wasn't my boyfriend, I thought, I was far too "fat" and insecure for a popular, good-looking guy like him. The rest of that summer evening was torture as I tried to pretend the hurtful comment didn't matter. I put on a happy face and consoled myself with too many cocktails while inside I was mortified and sickened at what happened. I remember looking around the university bar that evening at the seemingly naturally thin girls, bursting with confidence, wondering why I couldn't be like them. Why did I have to struggle with my weight and obsess about dieting, only to end up gaining more weight? What was I doing wrong? Why was I so flawed? I remember thinking that it was futile, I was

just going to be an insecure fat girl forever; that was my lot in life... Boy, was I wrong!

17 years later, after more heartache and struggle than I care to remember, and after being on every diet known to man, I decided I had had enough. I decided to quit looking for the next quick fix and find the truth about why I couldn't lose weight peacefully and permanently. I researched, found the tools, hired a coach and quit dieting. I sit here today in my ideal body. I've become a marathon runner and a weight loss coach with the tools and truth on how you too can find thinner peace and create your ideal body. The following principles are based on my personal experience, my coaching clients' journeys, and are inspired by the work of Martha Beck, Brooke Castillo, Byron Katie, Renee Stephenson and the dozens of other self-help and motivational books I have read and listened to. Read on for a step by step guide to creating your ideal body.

Ideal Body Principles

Principle One:
Knowledge is Power: Understanding your brain on a diet.

Have you ever seen a happy person on a restrictive diet? I haven't, and I certainly wasn't happy in my years of dieting. Recent research has shown that severely restricting calories causes: irritability, anxiousness, depression, binging, and an obsession with food. My hunch is that you don't need a controlled university study to tell you that – all you have to do is ask your friends what you are like on a diet. Look back and recall what you were thinking and feeling.

When we look at an external diet plan to tell us when and what to eat, we are overriding our animal instincts. We have been designed to eat when we are hungry, stop when we are satisfied, and store food for later consumption. By ignoring hunger and satiety signals and giving up desirable forbidden foods, we end up triggering a stress response in the brain and body. Martha Beck refers to this stress response as Famine Brain. Famine Brain can be activated by chronic dieting or even the expectation of food restriction. Therefore, just the idea and thought of going on a diet can create an obsession with food, feelings of anxiousness, irritability and the inability to feel satisfied after eating.

Numerous studies have also linked chronic stress with weight gain. The stress hormone cortisol is released when our body is under stress; this has been shown to slow down our metabolic rate and increase our cravings for sweet and salty foods. Excessive stress is also linked to greater levels of abdominal fat and increased risk of diabetes. Want to increase your stress level? Start a restrictive diet, cut out entire food groups or start obsessing about your appearance at your upcoming reunion.

The first principle to creating your ideal body is to really understand how your brain and body are affected by dieting. When you focus on dieting and ignore your hunger cues, you trigger famine brain and the result is often that you crave more processed foods, eat more than you need, burn less calories and store more fat. Our biological stress response cannot tell the difference between an imagined threat – i.e. bikini season and impending fad diet – or the real deal, upcoming famine and drought!

The good news is that we don't have to induce famine brain to lose weight. In fact, the opposite is true. If we lay the foundation for more peace and less struggle, we open ourselves up to the possibility of creating our ideal body – without struggle.

Principle Two:
Laying the foundation

I know what you are thinking, "How can I lose weight without dieting and restricting what I am eating? I'll just lose complete control and never reach my goals. It will be chaos!" I want you to open your mind to the possibility that by doing something different you will get a different result. Yes, you need to use up more calories than you take in to create your ideal body, but I believe that you can get there peacefully. We all have the ability to create our ideal healthy body. Dieting and overeating are learned behaviors that can be un-learned. You can get to your natural weight without diets or pills. In fact, the only long term solution to overeating is to never diet again. The other secret to long term weight loss is creating the right foundation.

Have you seen a naturally slender person eat? They are the people who often leave food, even dessert, on their plate without struggling. You know the type of person who stops mid-bite, because they are not hungry anymore or decides not to eat anything at an event because they are "not hungry" or "don't feel like eating." How do they do that? What's the difference between a person who seems to eat what and when they want while staying thin and a person who is trapped in a nightmare of counting calories and fat grams? Their foundation – their inner world – is made up of a different mindset or blueprint.

We all live in two domains: the inner world and the outer world. Our outer world is composed of the actions we take, the results we have and the physical things we create and engage with. Our inner world is made up of our thoughts, beliefs, and feelings. In order for us to create anything in the outer world, we have to first have a vision or thought about it in our inner world. Anything that we have or do in our outer world started first in our inner world, in our thoughts and mind. If you have extra weight on your body – if you overeat and use food as a coping strategy – it starts in your inner world and manifests in your outer world. Always.

A person who has an ideal body mindset or blueprint in their inner world can create and live it in their outer world, without struggle. This is one of the biggest reasons why they stay at their ideal body without much effort in their outer world.

The connection between your blueprint and your weight.

If you have ever been on a diet, watched others diet when you were younger, or heard messages about losing weight being hard work, then the chances are you have a blueprint that sets you up for struggling with your weight. My old and unhealthy blueprint was full of unhelpful messages like, "I'm very big boned, dieting and losing weight is hard work, maintenance is even harder, you need to be very careful about what you eat," and my personal favorite, "I'm lazy and hate exercise." Can you see how walking around with that blueprint I was bound to struggle and regain any weight I lost?

What does your blueprint say?
It's critical to your success to understand what messages are embedded in your blueprint so that you can change

them into ones that allow for weight loss and creating your ideal body. To find out what your blueprint says take out a piece of paper and answer the following questions:

1. To be at my ideal body weight I would like to lose ____ pounds.

2. Complete the following sentence:
   I have ____pounds of extra weight on my body because:
   i) ex. I overeat at night.
   ii) I don't exercise enough.
   iii)
   iv)

   (List at least five reasons.)

3. Write each reason across the top of your page and underneath each reason write the word "Why" at least 5 times.

Then ask your self "The Five Whys." Here is an example:

Reason: I overeat at night.
   Why?
   I like the taste of sweets and I have no self- control.
   Why?
I am addicted to sugar and I can't help myself when it's in front of me or in my house.
   Why?
   I'm weak and I have no willpower.

This person has a blueprint that says they are weak and have no willpower. The other piece of this blueprint is an underlying belief that they need willpower to not eat sweets.

By working with a coach, you can discover all sorts of hidden agendas in your blueprint.

You can also find these on your own by completing an exercise like this and by asking yourself what your barriers in the past have been. If your inner world consists of chronic thoughts and subconscious beliefs such as: "I'm weak and I have no willpower," that will manifest in your outer world as excess weight and lack of self-control. Any time you try to behave in a way that is contrary to your blueprint, you will feel very uncomfortable and find yourself struggling.

Brainstorm a list of other reasons why you believe you cannot lose weight permanently and peacefully.

_____

_____

_____

_____

Once you have a list of the beliefs and thoughts in your blueprint, you need to start dissolving them and creating new more healthy thoughts for your blueprint. Remember, everything in your physical world is the result of your thoughts and what you focus on in your mind. The right mindset for losing weight is the key to your success.

4. Dissolving your belief: You can start dissolving your unhealthy blueprint on your own by writing the limiting thought down, writing the opposite to it down

and then list the reasons why the opposite may be more true. For example:

a) Limiting thought or belief:

I am weak.
I have no willpower.
I always fail.

b) State the Opposite of limiting thought or belief:

I am strong.
I am powerful.
I will be successful.

c) List 5 Reasons why this opposite belief may be true:

I am strong may be true because:

1. I have lived on my own.
2. I take care of my family by chopping wood and shoveling snow.
3. I have delivered children.
4. I don't overspend my money.
5. I have been through hard times and I am still here.

d) You can then find a thought that feels better and think that when you have a desire to give up on your goals or overeat.

Better Thought may be: I am strong in many areas of my life and I do not need willpower to lose weight. I have what it takes to be successful, I can choose not to eat.

You want to start planting a seed of doubt in your mind that what you have believed may not necessarily be true.

A great tool for dissolving beliefs – or what I call your blueprint – is The Work of Byron Katie. See her website, www.thework.com for instructions. There are other valuable resources available or you can work with a Martha Beck Certified Coach skilled in dissolving beliefs.

30 days to a new ideal body blueprint!

What if I told you that in 30 days you could be feeling more peaceful about food and your body and be on your way to creating your ideal body? It's possible with the right blueprint and inspired action.

If you are willing to create a new, ideal body blueprint and focus on it for 30 consecutive days, you will be well on your way to your goals and taking the inspired action needed to prove it true.

The secret to creating your ideal body blueprint is to love yourself today at your current weight and to believe that your body can guide you towards your natural weight. You have to believe it is possible. You must also feel good when you think about your goals and your new blueprint. It may be helpful to get a small journal or notebook to start creating your ideal body blueprint in. To get started answer the following:

Step #1: Know what you want.

Be very clear about what exactly you want to achieve. Describe in a few sentences exactly what you intend to create: i.e. *I intend to create a lean and healthy body peace-fully and permanently.*

_____

_____

_____

Step #2: You have to see it and believe it, to achieve it.

Bring up an image of yourself at your goal. See yourself in your mind's eye as vividly as you can. Your brain cannot tell the difference between something you vividly imagine and something that has actually happened in the real world. The more you can see, feel, and experience your ideal body the more likely you are to move towards it.

I want you to imagine that you have achieved what you wanted. You're there. It's exactly as you imagined. It's perfect. If you have any doubt pop into your mind, slide it away and focus on your outcome as if you are already there.

Complete the following sentences as if you were already there, at your ideal healthy body:

a) I love living in my ideal body and I know I am there **because I** see:
(the joy in my face, my clothes fitting nicely, a certain number on the scale, etc.) _____

_____

_____

_____

b) I love living in my ideal body and I know that I am there because **I am easily taking action such as:**

(eating healthy foods, walking, etc.)_____

_____

_____

_____

_____

c) I love living in my ideal body and I know that I am there because **I** feel: (motivated, energized) _____

_____

_____

_____

_____

d) I love living in my ideal body and I know that I am there because **I hear others saying**: *(How did you do it? You look great.)* _____

_____

_____

_____

_____

e) I love living in my ideal body and I know that I am there because **I hear myself thinking:** *(I am so proud of myself, I feel so good!)* _____

_____

_____

_____

_____

Step #3: Making it meaningful

Your new blueprint needs to make sense in order for your subconscious to accept it. Once you start to believe in the possibility of this new blueprint, feel good about it, and commit to focusing on it daily you will be well on your way to creating it in real life.

Please use the information from the earlier exercises to create your new ideal body blueprint:

Blueprint template:

It feels great to have created a: *(insert goal from step #1) and*

I love that I am easily: *(insert #2B)*

It makes complete sense that I am seeing: (#2A).

I enjoy hearing others saying: (Step #2D) which is further

evidence that I am exactly where I want to be.

There is no doubt that I feel: (Step #2C)

because I believe that I: (new belief from 7B)

My thoughts that: (Step #2E)

match my success and I am so grateful for being here, living in my ideal body.

Write out your new ideal body blueprint into one succinct paragraph as if you were already there. For example:

It feels great to have created a healthy, fit body and I love that I am easily eating well and exercising. It makes complete sense that I am seeing the joy in my face and my clothes fitting nicely. I enjoy hearing others say: "How did you do it?" and "You look great!" which is further evidence that I am exactly where I want to be. There is no doubt that I feel energized and motivated because I believe that I am strong, powerful and can be successful. My thoughts that I am so proud of myself and I feel so good match my success and I am so grateful for being here, living in my ideal body.

As you read and create your blueprint, fine tune it until if flows and feels good! The key to anchoring this new foundation is to spend time every day focusing on it. The best way to do this is to develop a daily practice of visualization or journaling. I suggest the following:

Homework:

a) Begin a new journal that focuses only on your goal. Give it a great title such as "My Ideal Body Journal." The purpose of this journal is to anchor your foundation and new blueprint. Your job is to write in it every day as if you were already at your goal. You can start your journal by writing your ideal body blueprint out. After that, use your imagination and write at least one page a day on how wonderful and easy it feels to be in your ideal body. Even though you may not believe it at this point, have fun and for the few minutes that you are journaling see if you can feel the freedom of being there.

b) You may consider reading Jeanette Maw's *Pray Rain Journaling Book* available at www.goodvibecoaching.com for more information on how to incorporate this type of journaling into your daily practice.

c) For at least the next 30 days, as you wake in the morning and as you fall asleep at night, spend time thinking about your new blueprint. Visualize your-self at your goal, feeling peaceful, feeling ease, and enjoying being ideal body.

d) Take inspired action! The more time you spend feel-ing positively about your goal, the more you will feel inspired to take action. Use the Habits in the next set of Principles as a guide.

Principle Three:
How to become the Body Whisperer

Our body gives us clues all day long as to what it needs: food, water, sleep, etc. If we've spent a lot of time dieting and ignoring these signals, we may have turned down the volume on these cues. In order to create your ideal body, you need to begin hearing what your body is telling you and then take right action.

For me this was a new concept. I used to eat more by the clock and my emotions than for true hunger, and the turning point in my permanent weight loss journey was being very clear about the difference between emotional hunger and physical hunger.

You can start to learn the difference between emotional and physical hunger by becoming the body whisperer. Listen for that whisper of physical hunger. The difference can feel subtle at first. Just before you are about to eat, create a pause in the moment right before you want to eat and ask yourself if you are truly physically hungry – or is this an emotional hunger? Being emotionally hungry often comes on very quickly and has a feeling of anxiousness with it. There is sometimes a sense of urgency and we tend to go for processed foods when we are emotionally hungry. Spend some time, even a week, just noticing your eating, without judging it. Observe yourself, be curious, and start learning to tune in and become your own body whisperer.

The next crucial step is to learn to eat when you are hungry and stop when you are nicely satisfied not full. One big difference between naturally thin people and people who struggle with their weight is that naturally thin people eat when they are hungry and stop when they are satisfied. They feel uncomfortable when they are full and rarely eat past satisfaction.

We all were born with the skill of listening to hunger cues and satiety levels but sometimes lose it along the way. To re-learn this behavior, you may want to use a hunger scale.

Imagine that your hunger level is on a scale ranging from –5 to +5 with 0 being neutral. –5 being very hungry and +5 being overly full.

Hunger and satiety levels can be described as:

-1 slightly hungry, I am thinking about eating.
-2 hungry, I would like to eat something.
-3 more hungry, I really would like to eat something.
-4 uncomfortably hungry, I need to eat now, I am uncomfortably hungry.
-5 very hungry, I feel like I would eat anything put in front of me, I can't wait.

0 Neutral, I don't feel hungry or full

+1 I am not hungry anymore, but still want to eat.
+2 I am satisfied but could still eat more.

+3 I am satisfied and if I eat anymore I will be too full.
+4 I am overly satisfied and slightly uncomfortable.
+5 I am overly full, I feel physically uncomfortable

-5	-4	-3	-2	-1	0	+1	+2	+3	+4	+5

Very   **Neutral**   **Overly**
Hungry   **Full**

Use the hunger scale as a guide to get back in touch with your hunger cues. Always eat when you are hungry, –2, and stop when you feel satisfied, +2. Even if your hunger does not line up with mealtimes, you can eat a small amount of food to bring you to 0 or +1 so that you will be hungry again, -2, for meal times.

When you allow yourself to get too hungry, past –2, you may trigger emotional eating or overindulgence, i.e. famine brain.

When you are hungry, eat foods you want. Drop the diet food and really listen to what you want to eat. You may find initially you are drawn to junk food or treats but over time and once those foods are accessible, you may find yourself being drawn to foods your body requires, such as fruit and vegetables. Aim to eat between 5-7 servings a day, to help your body regenerate and function properly. If you are not losing weight using the hunger scale, increase your fruit and vegetable servings. Crowd out unhealthier choices, but always eat when you are hungry.

You may want to journal your food and hunger levels for a few weeks to learn more about your hunger, eating habits, and emotional eating triggers. You can journal your hunger and satiety levels, what you ate, and any strong emotional feelings or thoughts you had. Working one on one with a weight loss coach can help you address the emotional eating you may notice.

Here is a sample food journal:

Food	Hunger Level	Satiety Level	Feelings	Thoughts
Cereal Milk Orange Coffee	−3	+2	calm	Nothing significant
Donut (at work)	0	+3	anxious	It's not fair that I am overweight, I don't want to miss out on this good tasting treat. I don't care about eating healthy.

This person's journal leaves clues about why they eat when they are not hungry: negative self talk and an unhealthy blueprint. This person would benefit from addressing these thoughts with a weight loss coach or by learning to manage their thinking. The food journal and the hunger scale can be life changing for those ready to dig deep and look at their eating habits. Journaling is a critical first step to success.

To create your ideal body you need to incorporate new habits. These habits allow you to stop dieting and obsessing about your weight while bringing you to your ideal body weight. It is important that you begin thinking, acting and feeling in ways as if you were already at your ideal body weight. The body will follow the mind. Every week choose one or two habits to practice and incorporate into your new lifestyle. To learn more about how to incorporate these habits go to www.erinpostle.com.

Ideal Body Lifestyle Habits

1. I eat when I am hungry and stop when I am feeling satisfied. I don't skip meals or deprive myself. I eat at –2 on my hunger scale and stop at +2 or +3. I journal my food intake and hunger levels from a curious place, to help me learn about what hunger and satiety feels like and to notice emotional eating trends.
2. I eat food I want. Most of the food I eat is healthy and wholesome, I crowd out unhealthy processed foods gradually and I eat between 5-7 servings of fruit or vegetables per day.
4. I exercise on a regular basis for health and for increased feelings of well-being. I focus on how good I feel after I exercise. I aim for 10,000 steps per day.
5. I cope with stress in a variety of ways. I don't use food to comfort me. I use deep breathing, positive self-talk, meditation, and /or coaching to cope. I feel my feelings and don't use food to cover up emotions.
6. I occasionally enjoy eating and drinking for the mere pleasure of it. I savor pleasurable foods I choose to

eat. I eat them for their taste and not to deal with uncomfortable feelings. I don't feel guilty after I choose to eat something for pleasure.
7. I live in the moment and observe my thoughts, feelings, and behaviors. I take time for personal reflection, reviewing my healthy blueprint and focusing on gratitude for my body.
8. I take responsibility for my life and my happiness. I do not rely on food or others to fill me up.
9. I feel optimistic about my body and health. I do not beat myself up if I make a poor choice. I move forward without putting myself down. I learn more about myself from these experiences. I am not pre-occupied with food and dieting.

Principle Four:
What are you really hungry for?

Often times when we are obsessed with dieting and weight loss we fail to address or engage fully in all areas of our life. We spend hours focusing on that instead of our relationships, dreams, and desires. My overweight past was filled with countless hours of missed opportunities, wall-flower moments, and holding myself back until I "lost the weight." What a rip off!

I notice similar trends with my individual clients. They have spent lifetimes sitting on the sidelines, or they don't speak their mind because they believe they are unworthy at their current weight. They stop taking action towards their dreams and put their happiness on hold until they can drop the weight. The result is that they feel even more frustrated and unworthy because they are not living the life they want. When I was trapped in this cycle, I believed that I couldn't be free or express myself until I was at my ideal weight. I was hungry for self-expression and freedom and I used food to "fill me up" which pushed me further away from my goals and the freedom I desired.

Once you realize what your unmet needs are, you can take action towards fulfilling them without food. You can move forward from a clean place. To discover your unmet needs, try asking yourself "Why do I want...?" like this:

Why do I want to create my ideal body?
Because: *My clothes don't fit.*

Why do I want my clothes to fit?
Because: *So I can look better.*

Why do I want to look better?
Because: *I feel insecure in crowds and self-conscious of my weight.*

Why do I want to feel secure and less self-conscious?
Because: *I want to meet new people and be myself.*

Why do I want to meet new people and be myself?
Because: *I am lonely and I can't be myself.*

What are my unmet needs? What am I really hungry for?
I am hungry for feeling connected with others and for being myself.

You can see that underneath the goal of losing weight is an unmet need to connect with others and to be myself.

Feeling connected and important cannot be solved with food.

An emotional issue, a need, or something in our inner world can't be solved with something in the external world. The only way to solve an emotional problem or unmet need is to change our thoughts and beliefs – and then take action.

There are a number of excellent tools available to do this such as Brooke Castillo's *Self Coaching 101* or Meadow DeVor's *Take Happiness Lessons*. You can also work with a coach on how to change your chronic thinking patterns.

As you remove food as a cover for your unmet needs you may be inclined to take action. Here are some examples from my own life and from some of my clients:

- The need to be heard: standing up for yourself at work and in relationships, writing and expressing yourself on paper.
- The need for self love: putting yourself on your to-do list, following through on your personal commitments.
- The need to be free and have fun: taking up skating lessons, running, creative arts, sewing, dancing.
- The need to be loved: reaching out to others, calling friends, engaging in social activities, taking the first step towards a new relationship.

These new actions may feel strange or uncomfortable at first, but as you practice them you will begin to feel more confident and they will become part of your new and healthy blueprint. You may start defining yourself in different ways such as "I am an artist," "I am a woman who loves to dance," "I am a woman who takes care of herself first and others second."

Sadly, many of us waste years of our life waiting for the weight to come off before we start fully living. I recently held a live seminar and spoke to a woman in her 60's who broke down and sobbed about the missed opportunities in her life. She said she was ready to stop waiting for her weight to change before living her life. She had spent 40 years of her life waiting and the time never came. My guess is that the more she takes risks and starts living fully, the more joy and fulfillment she will feel and the less she will need food to fill her up.

I want you to know that you don't have to wait 40 years to take action and feel better.

You can start today. You don't have to start a restrictive diet or feel stress. You do have to dissolve your old blueprint and create a new ideal body blueprint. You can have lots of fun imagining yourself as your new ideal body and taking inspired action. You do need to take action: try out some of the Ideal Body Habits. Start filling your life up with other things beside food and meet some of your unmet needs today.

Don't wait. The time is now, struggling with weight is not your lot in life – and you too were not meant to be the insecure fat girl!

CƷ

To my sister Angela, who is an example of what is possible.

Erin Postle, M.Ed., Certified Coach & Counselor, is an accomplished coach who helps women who are frustrated and preoccupied with their weight. She takes them through a step by step process to develop the mindset needed to create and love their ideal body. What sets Erin apart is that she utilizes the latest coaching methods that she herself used to successfully reclaim her ideal body and her freedom. She can help you lead a more fulfilling life by teaching you to let go of your weight and your struggle. Contact her today for your free 30 min session at http://www.ErinPostle.com

ೞ

Escape from Mini-Van Madness

by Mary Ann Lowry, M.Ed.

At three o'clock, Meagan left the office where she worked as a dental assistant.

As she was saying "Good Bye," she announced to her co-workers that it was, "Time to Go to Work." Actually, she saw work as a place to relax and enjoy the camaraderie of her colleagues, as her "kick back" time.

Meagan appears to have a raging case of "Mini-Van Madness." When she leaves work, the remainder of her day revolves around shuttling her children to their various activities. Monday and Wednesday, Joe is involved in a karate class from 2:00 to 5:00 p.m. Sara takes ballet at 3:00 and then has to go to Kerry's house at 5:00 p.m. to work on a project for the history fair at the middle school. That's just a small glimpse into her schedule. The remainder of the week, including Saturday, is devoted to her children's extra-curricular activities.

As she turned on the car ignition, she mentally reviewed the activities for the remainder of the day to determine when they should eat dinner and, more importantly, what to eat for dinner. She estimated that they could eat at 7:00 p.m. and then remembered the church committee meeting to plan the Women's Retreat was also scheduled for that evening. Her commitments for the remainder of the day would be over around 10:00 p.m. that evening.

Although you may have never met Meagan, you might actually have a great deal in common. Do you think that your presence in your children's lives involves being present as you drive them to their various after school activities? Are you listening or asking about their day at school and what's happening in their lives, while serving as their private chauffeur for ballet class, soccer practice, and church youth group activities, etc. etc.? Do you feel like you should sell your home and live in an RV, so you can be home more often?

You aren't alone. Through my coaching practice I've worked with women who are trying to do it all. Their life activities are a reality for many women, who are parents of children from preschool age to the teen years. Their lives represent examples of a syndrome that I've labeled as "Mini-Van Madness." Can you identify with their stories?

When I included the syndrome and its name in a holiday letter, I received a great deal of feedback in response to that description, "Mini-Van Madness." Friends from far away, who I kept up with annually, told me that they knew this "Movement" very well, as they also found themselves behind the wheel of a mini-van, SUV, or any moving vehicle, between the hours of 3:00 to 6:00. Going home didn't offer much relief, because they needed to prepare dinner and help their children with their homework.

Do you find yourself thinking that the Moms who made sure their children had the opportunity to take ballet or be involved in sports, are the so-called "good mothers?" You may be surprised, but many of these "Good Mothers" have admitted in secret how tired they were. Your perception of what makes a "Good Mom" may not be accurate.

As I talk to exhausted clients, I reminded myself of the time when I was happy when confined to bed with the flu. I hated the side effects of the flu. Yet, the idea of being forced to rest was such a welcome respite. Even the best mothers can't do it all, while dealing with the flu. This was an escape clause that gave me permission to drop out of the madness for a day or two.

The truth is I didn't need an escape clause. You don't need an escape clause either. We're actually trapped in a wall of perceptions about what being a great mother is all about. I've learned a great deal and gained fresh insights, since my youngest son left for college in 2004. There are many ways to escape from "Mini-Van Madness" and it truly isn't about hoping to wake up with a bad cold or the flu.

After I said my good-byes in the dorm room to Ross, my youngest son, I checked into a local hotel before returning home. I decided to take a nap before thinking about having lunch or dinner. My nap turned into a 14 hour sleep-a-thon. When I woke up, it was 5:00 a.m. and I was still fully dressed with contacts still intact on my pupils. I returned to bed to read after taking out my contacts and slept until 11:00 a.m. After all those years of parenting while in motion, I was clearly a "Worn Out Woman," who had ignored my depleted energy supply for years.

Is it possible that you might also be a worn-out woman, who just might need to step away from the Mini-Van Madness that seems to be associated with the vision of being a "good mother?"

One easy way to assess whether you might be trapped in "Mini-Van Madness" is to take a good look inside your mini-van. Does it look like you just took it in and had it thoroughly cleaned and detailed? On the chance that you recently took your car in for a thorough spruce-up job, how long does it stay clean?

Play the role of an anthropologist, who is doing a study on life in 2009, and write down conclusions that an inspection of your mini-van or vehicle of choice might elicit. Would an investigation of your schlepping car possibly yield the following report 1000 years from now?

> During the first decade of the 21st century,
> people appeared to live in their cars. Though
> the paper is faded, there appear to be signs that
> food was gathered via their cars. Inhabitants
> of vehicles could acquire food boxed up and
> wrapped without ever leaving their cars. After
> thorough investigation, the flakes found on
> the floor of the car appear to be food crumbs.
> Vehicles were regarded as second homes, as
> various forms of clothing were found within the
> car that was recently discovered by archeologists.

Write three more conclusions that an anthropologist might deduce about our society based on the contents of your mini-van and/or SUV, as it looks today.

1.

2.

3.

4.

Write four adjectives that describe the inside of your mini-van.

1.

2.

3.

4.

Write four adjectives that describe your emotional state at the end of the day.

1.

2.

3.

4.

What messages is your body sending you at the end of the day? (i.e. energized or fatigued, etc.)

1.

2.

3.

4.

Refer to the comments you made about the interior of your car, as it is today. The adjectives you listed are actually a possible reflection of the state of your mind today. Do you see a theme related to the descriptions you listed about the interior of your car?

How does the anthropologist assessment of your mini-van or SUV tie into the adjectives that you listed on the proceeding page?

Do you see a relationship between your stress level and the state of your mind, as indicated by the interior state of your car? Describe any connections that you see between the interior of your vehicle and your inner state of wellness both emotionally and physically. Do you see a theme or a connection? If so write it below.

When I ask my clients who are seeking coaching for balance between parenting/life/work, there is usually a strong connection. For example, their mini-van is full of backpacks, track shorts, and a change of shoes, dead hamster in a shoe box in route to burial... and dog biscuits. I truly think I've heard of every random object that might be found in cars driven by Moms.

Now here's the wake-up call: The inner state of your car often reflects the inner state of your emotional health and physical wellness.

As long as the car runs, what difference does it make? Think of this in terms of yourself... as long as I have the time and the kids want to be in these activities, then I will be available. In my own life I learned the hard way, that my health was deteriorating, as I was pushing to fit in more and more. My body finally stopped the madness.

I'm writing this chapter, so you can understand that being caught in "Mini-Van Madness" really does put you at risk. Sorry, but you can't do it all. If you find yourself weary and ready to go to sleep at an early hour, your body is talking and wants you to listen. You don't have to continue to live as a "Worn Out Woman." There is hope for better days to come. If you identify with the relationship between the contents of your vehicle and your level of stress of fatigue, keep reading. There are answers just waiting for you, as you turn the page.

Understanding the Reasons Leading to the Problem

Reptilian Thinking Regarding Being a "Good Mother"

The brains of all living creatures are wired for survival. If a bear is threatened in the wild, he will either fight or run away (flight) from the source of the danger. When the danger is over, the bear can chill out. Most living creatures actually have the blessing of no language. They don't have to obsess about the event and project others' opinions about how they should have handled the situation. A friend reminded me that we never hear of a dog, who committed suicide. True? Our pets aren't weighed down with the burden of language (the non-stop inner chatter that infuses all kinds of thoughts in the mind).

You have the same brain wiring for survival. We need this instinct when we're facing a real danger. However, the danger you might be facing could be the opinions of others. Your dog, on the other hand, is free from worries about the opinions of others. As long as your pet has your TLC, then all is well. In fact, have you ever noticed how dogs are even attracted to the one person who doesn't care for animals? Your brain isn't wired like that, because women have plenty of language neurons in the brain.

You've lived long enough to have a strong idea of what a "Good Mother" does. You may be basing your values on the opinions of others and not on what is absolute truth. You put pressure on yourself to make sure that you're doing your part, so your children can have opportunities for enrichment.

Who said your children need to be part of all of these activities? With language thrown into the mix, your body may see this as a time to put the survival reptilian brain to work. However, the danger is only based on your perceptions of what being a "Good Mother" involves. Your body doesn't know the difference, so you carry this load that can be translated into a mild headache, tight shoulders, ongoing fatigue, chronic forgetfulness, etc. These are messages from your body that you are not living according to your own unique style and values. You are living from a social perception of what one should do to be a "Good Mother."

Here are some examples of thoughts related to the pressure of performing as the "Good Mother":

"My kids won't have the same opportunities as their friends if I don't enroll them in all these extra-curricular opportunities."

"Karate is good for Johnny. We don't want to raise a kid vulnerable to bullies."
"My kids need the structure that numerous after school activities provide."
"I want my kids to be faithful Christians, so they need to go to every youth group activity."

Even when money is tight, parents feel the burden to continue to give their children opportunities for enrichment. That's not a bad thing. However, anything done to excess can suddenly lose its charm. Chocolate cake is a great wonderful blessed treat in my opinion. There is everything to like and even love about chocolate cake. However, the chocolate cake becomes a source of grief, if we decide to eat the whole cake solo. The cake may weigh three pounds, but that translates to ten pounds on my body. Go figure!?

The Trap of "I Have to"

You truly don't have to do anything that you don't want to do. However, you can choose to do things you want to do. To say those words, as if you have no other life choices, can keep you feeling shackled. They take your freedom away. Do you honestly, truthfully have to keep up the pace to fill each minute with a worthy structured activity? Many Moms have told me "I have to sit with Billy to do his homework, so he will make good grades." Do Moms really have to do this? Do you really need to drive your children to five different birthday parties every week-end?

Formulas for Escaping Mini-Van Madness

Deal with the Good Mother Perceptions

Remember that it's the language messages that we feed ourselves that lead to the thoughts that drive our behavior. If you take the time to reflect on a thought to see if it really is true, you may be surprised. An absolute truth applies to everyone and everything. Would you tell your best friend that she needed to drive her children to five different birthday parties on Saturday to be considered a "Good Mother?" I would guess your answer is no and that means that the thought in your head is probably not absolutely true. This is a great test to see if your thought is true. If you wouldn't tell anyone else to rise to your expectations for yourself, then the language center of your brain has played a trick on you and you bought into it.

Change Your Thinking

Rather than advising you to think differently, I'm going to share a bit of wisdom from my colleague, Brooke Castillo. Brooke wrote a book and developed a coaching model called "Self-Coaching 101. In essence the "Self-Coaching" allows you to become your own life coach. It's based on five different questions to ask yourself.

1. What is the circumstance (the reality)?
2. What is your thought?
3. What feelings do you have related to that thought?
4. What actions do your feelings prompt you to choose?
5. What are the results of this action?

This is a great model to follow whenever you have a negative emotion like fear, jealousy, anxiety, or anger. If you aren't in immediate danger, the chances are that you need to take a mental inventory to change the thought that caused the chaos.

The following is an example of how to apply the "Self Coaching 101 Model" to your perception of what a "Good Mother" should do.

Circumstance: Matthew has to write a two paragraph essay for English homework.

Thought: I need to monitor Matthew and stay with him to see that the work is completed accurately.

Feeling: Tired, Frustrated, Food Craving Mode, Overwhelmed.

Action: Matthew continues to take his time writing the paragraph. You've promised him a reward when he finishes and that isn't doing the trick.

Result: You become so frustrated that you've landed right in the middle of a huge power struggle between you and your son.

Now let's use the same scenario with a different thought:

Circumstance: Matthew has to write a two paragraph essay for English homework.

Thought: Matthew has a choice to write his essay before the timer goes off or he will choose to lose his video game privileges for the remainder of the day.

Feeling: Empowered, Calm, Controlled, More Relaxed (Matthew can only control Matthew. Mom lets him choose the outcome for his behavior choice.)

Action: Matthew may or may not choose to do the essay before the timer goes off. However, he is in control of his decision.

Results: Matthew may initially suffer the consequence, as he realizes that you are serious about giving him the choice for the outcome of his behavioral choices. Matthew may decide that he really misses his video games and complete the assignment before the timer goes off.

The first thought would be an energy drainer. However, the second thought is like removing the chains that shackled you to your kitchen table and/or homework central.

Question the Words "I Have to" or "I Need to"

Remind yourself that you do have choices. You'll love the feeling of power that comes from having choices. According to Martha Beck, we have three other options besides completing a "have to" task:

You can bag it. Cancel obligations. Limit after school activities to only one per child.
You can better it. Discover activities that your children will truly enjoy that develop wellness and don't demand huge time commitments.

You can barter it. I would bet that you aren't the only devoted Mom, who would love a respite from spending your afternoons behind the wheel of a mini-van.

This is one of the reasons that carpools originated. This is an ancient ritual that was in place during my own childhood. Parents connect with other parents and work out a trade in driving responsibilities.

Listen to your body and complete an energy inventory of all your current activities.

Consider your energy level from a -10 to a +10 level. If an activity yields a score of -10, this means that you are totally drained and energy depleted. This is an indicator that you are feeling totally shackled. On the other hand, a score of +10 indicates that you find the activity freeing, energizing, and really in sync with your own unique wiring. Martha Beck recently developed a "Daily Thought Sanitation Exercise" to examine your "to do" lists. On the right hand of the column, please provide a number from -10 to +10, indicating how your "Body Compass" reacts to the thought of that particular "to do" item.

Items to do in the next 24 hrs	"Body Compass Rating"
Working on my IRS audit	−10
Taking a creative Writing Class	+8
Taking Scott to swimming practice and picking him up	−5
Taking Sarah to soccer practice and picking her up	−3
Preparing for the Women's Retreat Committee Meeting	−2

Watching "Steel Magnolias" for the 100th time on the movie channel	+9

If the "Body Compass" ratings are going in a negative direction, it's time to take a good hard look at the unpleasant things on your list. Hold in your mind the thought of doing the most unpleasant thing on your list. Allow your uncomfortable emotions to be as they are, without criticizing or judging. Notice the thoughts that come up in association with the event. Write the thoughts down and take some time to do some "Self-Coaching" with regards to each thought that causes feelings related to any type of emotional suffering, whether mild to severe. What underlying thought is truly upsetting you and is the root of your negative or gremlin emotion?

For example: *If I were a better mother, I would be less selfish and more giving to my children to make sure they receive what they need.*

(This underlying belief seems to be a real monster thought with layers and layers of underlying beliefs keeping it afloat and giving it so much power. Many parents who I coach privately are shackled by the desire to "act as good parents." This is a commendable desire, but it's too nebulous and actually too relative to get a clear fix on what is a "good parent?" It also is a thought that keeps parents captive. When that happens, I recommend hiring a Life Coach or doing your own self-coaching.)

Plan a Family Meeting to Determine What Activities Stay on the Agenda

If your children are old enough to process language, ask them to prioritize their "to do" list. When presented with this opportunity, my boys decided that all extra-curricular activities were on the negative side for them. They wanted to watch videos or play Nintendo rather then be involved in some type of physical fitness activity. That wasn't exactly what I had in mind as a trade-off, so I gave them a choice.

They weren't given the option of giving up physical fitness altogether, but they could decide to pursue another sport. They left swimming one spring and participated in track. Technically, they could have stayed active in both sports, but we decided as a family that the sacrifice of time was too great. Through a family meeting, we were able to talk it over and decide what activities were going to be ongoing and what activities we could eliminate from our "to do" list. Involving the children in the decision worked really well. They felt that they owned the decision.

Benefits of "Escaping Mini-Van Madness"

Freedom to Live Authentically as the Real You

In a time long ago in a galaxy far, far away, you may remember that in high school and college you lived on your terms. You weren't selfish or self-absorbed. However, you made time to fit in the activities that were important to you.

Your children are top priorities in your life now. Yet, you can still be the type of Mother that your children need and live authentically at the same time. When I became seriously ill during the years when my boys were in elementary school, I felt guilty. We had to eliminate activities, because I didn't feel like driving. I expected my boys to be very disappointed and tried to arrange for other rides. To my surprise they loved having my time and playing games together or watching videos together.

I followed a script for good parenting by putting the pressure on myself to take the boys to all their activities. I was following a good parenting formula, based on my own limiting thoughts. It took a life interruption to show me how faulty my thinking was.

As I recovered, I spent more time playing games with them and taking them to the park.

They loved having my time, and I truly enjoyed being with them as my true self.

Fill the Time with Activities That Fuel You

Your children's needs are a top priority during their formative years. However, research studies recently completed by UCLA looked at the way women handle stress. Most of the stress literature has focused on ways humans deal with stress. It appears that men and women actually have different coping mechanisms. To escape the fight/flight stress, women actually cope with stress by connecting and collaborating with other women.

I address this to women, since most women are the ones at home during the hours of Mini-Van Madness. This study found that when the hormone oxytocin is released as part of the stress responses in a woman, it buffers the fight or flight response and encourages her to tend to her children and gather with other women instead. Hanging out with your girlfriends while your children enjoy playdates is a great way for Moms to deal with the stress that comes with living.

As you're tending your children, who may be focused on one outside activity now, take the time to get to know the other parents involved in supporting their junior soccer player. Some of my closest friendships during the years that my boys were active were with the other mothers, whose children belonged to the same swim club. Initially, I would drop off the boys and run a multitude of errands. One day, I stayed and realized that I was missing out on the opportunity to get to know some really quality women.

Charge Your Batteries

Most people tend to parent as they were parented. Even though you may hear them say, "I will never act like my mother," it happens anyway. Model for your children the process of living with margin in their lives. Limit the number of extra-curricular activities and discuss this process in a family meeting.

Dr. Richard Swenson, the author of *Margin: Restoring Emotional, Physical, Financial, and Time Reserves to Overloaded Lives* makes a case for the fact that many of his patients come in with symptoms of stress or exhaustion. It seems that these people fill every minute to the max and there appears to be no way out. He uses the analogy of "Margin" to explain how we all need room for down time. He challenges his readers to think about whether they would purchase his book if every page were filled with all words and no "margin." Even the best book would look overwhelming, if every space is taken up by words.

Do you feel like I've got your number? As you're nodding in agreement with Swenson's description of "Margin," remember that the same holds true in every life, including your life. Scheduling time to do nothing will not only benefit the parents – it will also model healthier, stress-free living for your children. Studies have found that taking time for prayer and other spiritual disciplines fuels your spirit to cope with what life brings your way. You're teaching your children that "busy" is not the norm and making time for a quiet time or family game night is a priority.

Replenish Your Energy

You don't have to wait until your children are raised to begin to nurture and make plans to capture your heart's desire. Being there for your children does not have to involve "Mini-Van Madness." As you give yourself the freedom to "Escape from Mini-Van Madness," you'll note that you'll feel more energized. Your children may complain initially, but they'll get over it. By marking out huge chunks of time for nothing or a trip to the park to relax, you may very well see a new surge of energy and find that your children are happier.

It's worth a try to walk away from that trap. You'll never know what freedom and peace will result from changing your practice until you follow the steps to escape from "Mini-Van Madness." I urge you to slowly review your very full life now and begin to make slow strides toward living a life unshackled and free of strongholds. You are so worth the effort. By the way, your beloved family is also deserving of the time for planned "blissful nothingness."

Feel free to e-mail me for extra support if you need some guidance for "Escaping Mini-Van Madness." My wish for all parents is the opportunity to live a free, full, abundant life, while raising awesome children in the process. Contact me if I can be of help.

Go to my website to retrieve these tools: "Am I trapped in 'Good Mom' Syndrome?" and "Family Meeting Priority Worksheets" www.escapeminivanmadness.com

಄

Brent and Ross, I love you dearly and consider it a privilege to be your Mom. Your adult lives speak for themselves and give me the credibility to do what I love, Coaching Parents to Raise Awesome Kids.

Mary Ann Lowry, M.Ed. is a Martha Beck Certified Master Coach, who specializes in Coaching Parents based on her personal experience as a Mom and Educator. Her clients see immediate results with parenting challenges as she blends Martha Beck's coaching tools with her professional expertise. If you struggle with life/work/parenting balance, Mary Ann also offers coaching to help you transition to a more relaxed, stress-free lifestyle. Whether you need individual parental coaching or would benefit from group coaching classes, contact Mary Ann via e-mail to determine solutions for the most challenging family and/or parenting dilemmas.   maryannlowry@mac.com

Please see bibliography on p. 257.

CB

From Tragedy to Transformation

Finding the Gifts in Crisis

by Amy Johnson

Tragedy

"How strange that the nature of life is change, yet the nature of human beings is to resist change. And how ironic that the difficult times we fear might ruin us are the very ones that break us open and help us blossom into what we were meant to be." – Elizabeth Lesser

It's been said that change is the only constant. Life altering, transformational events are inevitable. At some point, everyone will experience a catalytic event that seems to throw their life off-course. Our lives are always on-course for greater things, but they can certainly feel off-course at the time. We feel lost and our identity may be threatened. We're thrust out of our routine, out of the life we had grown accustomed to, and are forced to reinvent some piece of our world. Although the pain, shock, and sense of loss that typically accompanies these events do eventually fade, we're never the same person we were before the event.

If you are in the midst of a transformational event, a "crisis" if you will, welcome to this chapter. Just reading this is a good sign! Facing your pain is the first step to receiving the gifts a crisis can bring. I want you to remember that literally everyone experiences crisis in one way or another. This Quest is the subject of countless fables and fairy tales, works of literature, Hollywood movies, and rock and roll ballads. It is metamorphosis – the journey back to wholeness after a transformational life event.

There is no right or wrong way to feel, think, or experience your journey and there is no possible way to *not* get through it. But learning to identify and examine your thoughts can make the journey quicker, less painful, and lead to a fuller experience. Ultimately, the experience you have is exactly the experience you are meant to have. Whatever challenges you face are exactly the teachers you need.

I use the term "crisis" in this chapter but as you will come to see, "blessing" or "opportunity" would be more appropriate. As painful as they are, I believe these episodes in our lives are nothing short of miracles – they are gurus from which we can learn more about ourselves and live a happier, fuller life than we ever could without them.

This chapter will outline a process for making peace with and finding meaning in crisis. I'll illustrate with examples from my own life and the lives of two clients*: Danielle, dealing with the loss of her dream job, and Maureen, faced with a debilitating illness. The process described here can be applied to any stressful life event, so you'll learn valuable tools you can apply to your own life to make peace with any situation and walk away with greater perspective. The steps to making it through crisis which will be discussed are:

- Accept the reality of where you are and learn to distinguish suffering caused by actual events from suffering caused by the stories we tell ourselves about the events.
- Once we've grieved the actual loss and identified the self-imposed pain, we can examine those limiting beliefs and choose thoughts that better serve us.
- There comes a point after the transformational event when you are ready to accept the mission of change you've been given. I will show you how powerful questions can help you open the gifts of crisis more quickly.

Pain

"The only way out is through." – Robert Frost

Life after a crisis is never the same as it was before. Sometimes this is true in a very obvious way, like after the death of a spouse or the loss of a job, and sometimes it's true in a more subtle way, like in the case of a medical diagnosis that requires a change in lifestyle, or the end of a meaningful relationship. In either case, change is often accompanied by a sense of loss for what was or what could have been.

It is valuable to determine whether suffering is caused by the actual catalytic event or from our own stories about the event. From Dr. Stephen Hayes' *Acceptance and Commitment Therapy*, clean pain is a direct effect of the event itself – it's the result of a very real loss. Dirty pain, on the other hand, is not directly due to the event but to the thoughts and the meaning we assign to what is happening. We may experience clean pain when our physical symptoms flare up or when our ex comes to pick up his belongings. Dirty pain, on the other hand, results from the thoughts we play over and over in our minds. For example, when my client Danielle's company restructured and she lost her dream job as an advertising executive, much of the sadness over the loss she experienced was clean pain. Danielle's belief that, "I'll never find another job as good as the one I lost," and her tendency to equate being unemployed with being hungry and homeless caused dirty pain. When another client, Maureen, was diagnosed with a painful and debilitating intestinal disease, her physical symptoms were clean pain. Maureen's projecting into the future about the possible state of her life and her health down the road was dirty pain. In other words, dirty pain includes the painful thoughts we have about reality, whereas clean pain involves our actual reaction to reality. Dirty pain, very biased and very optional, is responsible for the vast majority of our suffering.

Learning to distinguish clean pain from dirty pain after a crisis can be a giant step toward accepting what is and experiencing relief from suffering. Although the difference may seem clear in the examples above, in the midst of suffering the difference between what is real and what is perceived can be quite fuzzy. The ability to notice our thoughts from the standpoint of a neutral (if not compassionate) observer is critical. To this end, it's helpful to begin a mindfulness practice where we practice non-judgmentally observing our thoughts. I teach my clients to be the connoisseurs of themselves, acting like objective researchers studying a new species. Non-judgment is the key – they are watching their thoughts with pure curiosity, not believing them or taking them as truth. The fact is, our thoughts are not always true. They're often more akin to habits, habitual patterns of neurons that tend to fire together. When you can detach and notice your thoughts as they occur – rather than remaining wrapped up in believing them – you can easily see where your suffering is based on the event and where it's based on your thoughts about it.

How do we heal clean pain? Good old fashioned grieving. In grieving a loss, we let emotion wash over us, we bathe in it, take it in, and we slowly begin to heal. As Robert Frost said, "The only way out is through," and that's exactly what we need to do during the grieving process – go through to the other side. On the other side of pain is peace. Danielle needed to grieve the loss of her former career. Aside from her fear-based thoughts about the future and her overly romanticized memories of the past – which were causing her dirty pain – there was a real loss she could identify, sit with, accept it, and feel it all the way through. She grieved her identity as an advertising executive with her former firm and the rift in the friendships she had formed with co-workers. Through grieving, she was able to accept change and let go of her former identity. Through grieving these things and watching her thoughts, she began to see her dirty pain, too.

Inquiry

"The only time we suffer is when we believe a thought that argues with reality." – Byron Katie

Danielle had grieved her real losses and was left with a gaggle of dirty pain. "Yeah, I miss my old life and my colleagues and I can sit with that and let it heal. But I still have these persistent thoughts that the heyday of my career is over. I'll never have it as good as I had it with the firm. I was so happy there and now it's just gone. And that's just fear about my career status – what about my real survival? I do need to find more work soon or I could be in real financial trouble. What do I do with all of these beliefs?" My response: Question them.

Once you've identified the persistent thoughts that cause suffering, examine them one by one. We can choose to inquire into the truth of our thoughts and beliefs rather than automatically taking them as truth. The Work of Byron Katie is the best tool there is for questioning painful beliefs. The Work is a process of inquiry in which we shine a bright light on a hurtful belief and really examine the truth of that statement. The goal of The Work is not necessarily to have us give up or disbelieve our thoughts, but to find the reality and truth of the situation for ourselves.

Because detailed descriptions of The Work can be found in Byron Katie's books and at www.thework.com, I won't go into a detailed description of the four questions and turnaround statement that are the bedrock of the process. Instead, I'll use examples from work with Danielle and Maureen to highlight the power of this method for dealing with dirty pain.

Maureen was in her mid 40s, a married mother of four college-aged kids. Throughout her life, Maureen was always the person in charge. She was an extremely responsible, organized person who excelled at making plans, researching options, and pulling everything together in her own life and the lives of her family members. Before her illness, Maureen said her best quality was her ability to be in control and get things done. She was a person who emphasized action and results over relaxation and self-care. Maureen believed that anything optional she did for herself was selfish and overly indulgent, so most of her time was spent accomplishing things for others.

After a particularly stressful period while managing the remodel of her home, nursing her son through surgery and rehabilitation, and helping her husband find new work, Maureen developed a host of debilitating gastrointestinal problems. She was hospitalized for over two weeks which forced her to face her biggest fear – being bed-ridden and unable to take care of everything at home. Maureen finally had to admit that she did not have control over her body or her life at that moment.

The first few months after Maureen went home from the hospital were challenging. She felt completely robbed of her sense of control. Maureen found herself uncomfortable relying on others. Frequent doctor visits took over her schedule, and sometimes even her body was out of her control. There was a lot of emotional pain associated with her perceived loss of control. An important first step was separating the clean pain and the dirty pain. Maureen began to mindfully watch her thoughts and learned to not identify with them or instantly believe or act upon them. She compassionately noticed the habitual ways her brain fired in different circumstances and just let the thoughts go. This practice showed Maureen that she was something beyond her frenzied thoughts and actions – she was a wise soul inside a busy body and she was capable of observing the whole busy mess that used to be her life. This practice also helped her relax and spend time in the present, not bothered by to-do lists or plans for the future.

Maureen spent some time grieving the loss of her old way of life. As she sat through the clean pain, the dirty pain began to rise. "This is who I am, the person who does everything. Without that, I don't know who I am;" "I need to be in control or things will never get done;" "Life will be much more difficult if I am unable to keep things in line." We inquired into these thoughts one by one. For example, because Maureen had almost always gotten things done, she came to realize that she really couldn't know that it's absolutely true that if she's *not* in control, things will not get done. In fact, when she searched for examples of the opposite, she found them. She saw that when she was in the hospital, her family pitched in and took care of themselves. Although this certainly didn't eradicate her long-held belief, this realization opened a window of hope – the possibility that maybe her belief was not always true.

Maureen considered the next question in The Work, "How do you feel or react when you believe that thought?" After some deep inquiry into her own emotional and behavioral patterns she identified several reactions to the thought, "I need to be in control or things will never get done." Physically, her muscles became tense and she felt some adrenaline surge throughout her body, preparing her for the tasks at hand. Not surprisingly, she reported feeling most of the physical sensation in her stomach area – exactly where her medical issues had their center. Maureen realized that the thought was closely followed by other, similar thoughts about what it meant if she did not have things under control. In terms of behaviors, she would begin to make lists and experience something she called "tunnel-vision" where she became so focused on getting the task done that she became oblivious to the people around her. Maureen was shocked at how much impact this single thought had on her body and the way she behaved.

When Maureen considered the final question in the process, "Who would you be without this thought?" she really became conscious of the impact of this belief on her life. Without the ability to think, "I need to be in control or things will never get done," Maureen felt free, like the self-imposed shackles she had fastened around herself had been released. She could imagine how she might react with much more easiness and peace in so many situations in her life. She would not wake up in the middle of the night reciting her to-do list for the next day. She would not experience that awful feeling in her stomach. By looking for the truth of her situation, Maureen discovered a more peaceful way to think.

Next, we took the statement and turned it around to its opposite. Rather than, "I need to be in control or things will never get done," we looked at the statement, "I need to give up control or things will never get done." Maureen could immediately see some truth in this when she thought about her recent stint in the hospital and on bed rest at home. When she gave up control in those situations, albeit involuntarily, things did get done. Also, Maureen knew that if she didn't learn to give up control and live life with more ease and relaxation she was bound to suffer another health setback due to stress, again leaving her unable to get things done.

Transformation

"The pessimist sees difficulty in every opportunity. The optimist sees the opportunity in every difficulty." – Winston Churchill

Coaches ask a lot of questions. We believe that the answers are always available inside the client, although they may often feel buried and unrecognizable. Powerful questions are one tool a client can use to dig up the answers they're looking for.

After someone has grieved their losses and has identified and dissolved some of their dirty pain, they may be ready to consider the deeper lessons in the crisis. A powerful tool for uncovering those lessons is the question, "How is this situation perfect?"

Looking for the perfection in the situation shifts your focus so that you begin to consider the potential gifts in the crisis. To be clear, the word "perfect" does not imply that you would choose the situation if you were able to choose; it doesn't mean you are happy with the outcome or that you are necessarily glad it came about (although after grief subsides and a new perspective is taken, people are often very grateful the crisis occurred). The timing of this question is crucial – it would be simply cruel to ask a client how the death of their spouse or deterioration of their health was perfect too soon after the event. But when appropriate, asking how the situation is perfect is essentially asking, "How did this crisis teach you what you most needed to learn?" If you had to imagine that this situation was placed in your path specifically to benefit you in some way, what would that look like? Thinking about the circumstances in this way opens you to a completely new, previously inaccessible way of thinking.

"How is this situation perfect?" is a valuable question regardless of your own spiritual views or your personal beliefs about fate, destiny, or things happening for a reason. Through the challenges in my own life and my desire to make sense of them, I've come to believe that everything does happen for a reason and that we come to this earth with things we'd like to learn and experience in our lifetime. In my early 20s, the personal lesson I most needed to learn was that I didn't have to be perfect – I needed to learn how to give up the excessively high standards I set for myself.

I had just moved out of state, hours away from my family and friends, to enter a prestigious doctorate program in psychology. A reasonable goal would have been to make it through the five years of graduate school having grown as a person and learned a lot. Never one to be reasonable when it came to my own goals and standards, I was determined to be the best graduate student my program had ever seen, teaching and publishing more than anyone in the history of the program, all the while having an extremely full and active social life and contributing to the community. My behavior patterns reflected those goals and I was quickly stressed and exhausted. After a full year of an unbelievably busy schedule, my body let me know loud and clear that it had to end. I developed panic disorder and was having ten or more severe panic attacks every day. I became afraid to leave my apartment for fear of having an attack in public. I developed phobias about attending class (not to mention the classes I was teaching), exercising, driving, and being in groups of people. I lived alone and felt incapable of everyday tasks such as grocery shopping or making the two block trip to the library. The crisis forced me to slow down. It taught me to take care of myself, re-evaluate my standards, and listen to my body for what *felt* right rather than believing my thoughts about the person I needed to be. The two years I lived with panic attacks were my "dark night of the soul," but they were also my greatest teacher. I wouldn't trade those years for anything – they were the most direct and effective way of arriving at a place of peace and happiness where I can be truly kind to myself.

Since that time, I find that whatever I most need to learn shows up, often in the form of what appears to be a negative event. When I find myself lacking compassion – BAM! – There's a difficult co-worker who can only be dealt with through extreme compassion. When I'm lacking patience – POW! – Here comes a traffic jam or some more serious situation that demands patience. As the famous Buddhist quote goes, "When the student is ready, the teacher will appear."

So, my belief is that crisis teaches us lessons we could have never otherwise learned, or at least not in the same way, and adversity in itself bestows gifts of courage, determination, and strength we wouldn't have otherwise experienced. If this information goes against your own personal beliefs, *always* defer to what feels right to you. When you bypass your conditioned thoughts, get quiet and listen for what feels right. That answer you hear *is* your right answer. Even if what feels right to you is that life is a series of random events and there is no larger purpose, you can still contemplate how the situation is perfect and find the gifts in crisis. Once the crisis has occurred, wishing it hadn't, or cursing the randomness or unfairness in the universe, only adds to your suffering. Even if it doesn't feel right to believe that the situation came into your life for a purpose, now that it has occurred there may be some lesson you can take from it. Again, that doesn't automatically mean you'll consider it a blessing. It doesn't mean you'd choose it if you could, and it doesn't disrespect the relationship that ended, the body that used to function perfectly, or the friend or family member who died. It just puts you back in a position of responsibility for your life and in a place where you can find something good in something tragic.

When she was ready, Danielle – laid off when her dream job as an advertising executive was eliminated – began considering how losing her job may have been perfectly designed and delivered by the universe for a greater purpose. She first acknowledged the ways in which she had compromised herself for her previous job and the ways in which it was less than perfect. Although she loved the firm, there were complicated office politics that prevented Danielle from speaking her mind at times. Most of the time, this was bearable and she felt that the benefits of the job outweighed this cost. But there were times when it was more of an issue and left Danielle feeling unacknowledged and unable to be truly authentic. These feelings were beginning to affect her feelings about herself and the way she approached non-work related situations. Asking, "How is this situation perfect?" allowed Danielle to acknowledge some of the aspects of her job that were not perfect and helped with the overly romanticized view of the job she had when she first lost it.

Danielle talked about how much she has learned about the advertising industry as a whole through the process of looking for new work. There were many changes in the field that she had been unaware of when she was insulated safely within her former firm. Visiting a variety of firms gave her a broader picture of the way she really wanted to shape and guide her career as an exec. By the end of our work together, Danielle had a long list of the ways in which she could see the loss of her job as perfect. Most of all, she was growing in ways she otherwise wouldn't have and she no longer felt she had to stifle part of who she was. Danielle also confided that she had been dating a great new guy who she really saw a future with. They met at a local job seekers' group she had joined where members gave each other feedback on their resumes and allowed them to practice their interview skills. This great new relationship was just one more "perfect" outcome of the situation she once thought of as a tragedy.

The process of finding meaning in crisis for Maureen took a little longer, but ultimately had an even greater payoff. Maureen's illness taught her many things. She learned that it was okay to give up trying to control things, that they found a way of working out whether she managed the process or not. When she managed the process and tried to hold everything together, her GI tract let her know by acting up, forcing her to take a step back and surrender control. She is learning to take care of herself and she is learning to value peace and faith in the universe over personal action and getting things done.

Maureen discovered that her illness was perfect because it moved her, by leaps and bounds, closer to her greatest wish for herself – inner peace and happiness. Could she have realized her wish without going through the illness? We'll never know. Maybe it would have taken longer or maybe the lesson would not have been as clear. Maureen doesn't believe she would be as peaceful or happy as she is today without the crisis. By meditating on how the situation was perfect, Maureen came to understand that her illness was the perfect teacher for the lessons she most had to learn.

I also love asking clients, "How will this crisis transform you?" Considering how you want to change for the better after the experience gives a feeling of great power. It frees you from identifying with the role of the victim. As Danielle said, "Losing my job was perfect because I learned so much about the advertising industry and the type of career I want to design for myself that I never would have learned at my old firm. I am transformed in that I am choosing to embrace the part of me that refuses to be or say anything other than what's authentically me. I'm choosing to blaze my own trail in this field rather than let someone else put me in a box." Focusing on the positive changes in your life brings you to live in the present and begin dreaming about future possibilities. This begins the exciting process of "dreaming and scheming" – waking up to possibility after fighting to stay afloat in a pool of clean and dirty pain.

The Beginning

"Should you shield the canyons from the windstorms, you would not see the beauty of their carvings" – Elizabeth Kubler-Ross

By now, I hope the term "crisis" sounds like a flagrant misnomer. It certainly feels like a crisis at the time. Challenging, sometimes tragic events are part of the human saga. By grieving the losses and dissolving dirty pain, you can begin to view these crises as gifts in strange wrapping paper.

I love helping clients see that it's at their lowest point that they generate the energy to be catapulted to a higher place. Every act of spiritual growth or metamorphosis is preceded by a fall of one kind or another. It's when people are broken open, grieving their losses and recognizing dirty pain all around them, that they become more of the person they truly want to be. Whether the lesson they most need to learn is compassion, surrender, or patience, the adversity they experience is perfect in its ability to teach us the exact lessons we need in the best way possible. Elizabeth Kubler-Ross said, "Should you shield the canyons from the windstorms, you would not see the beauty of their carvings." The windstorms, or crises in our lives are necessary; they allow us to see beauty we wouldn't otherwise see. These are the gifts of crisis.

*: The clients' stories are used here with permission. In addition, their names have been changed to protect their privacy.

ଔ

I would like to thank Martha Beck and Byron Katie for making their insight and brilliance available to the world and changing many, many lives for the better. I would also like to thank "Danielle" and "Maureen" for allowing their stories to be told. Special thanks go to our editor, Anna Paradox, and the brilliant and generous co-authors of this book.

Amy Johnson is a psychologist and certified coach who helps clients navigate life transitions and find meaning in their crises. Her coaching examines the thoughts that cause suffering and eliminates the fears that hold people back in life. Amy has a doctorate in psychology and bases her methods on the latest brain research. She offers individual and group coaching and frequently leads workshops and seminars near her home in Chicago. For more information, visit Amy at www.dramyjohnson.com

Please see bibliography on p. 257.

ଔ

Ending the War at Work

by Dee Carrell, MBA

Feel that sharp stabbing pain between your shoulder blades as you slide behind your desk? Hit between the ears with an email missile even before you finish your double-mocha latte? Welcome to the workplace war games.

The office provides a perfect medium for nurturing toxic relationships. Competition, greed, fear, and a hearty splash of ego-run-amuck feed suspicion and hostility.

Contemporary wisdom suggests an array of tactics to derail office attacks. Most techniques involve email-sniping, rapid fire retorts, and amassing troops – your co-workers – in your corner to outsmart and outplay your opponent. The best defense is a good offense; you prepare for war.

You've experienced these bloodless battles. I know I have, often suffering a humiliating retreat at the hands of a skilled combatant. Embarrassed and powerless, I vow to get this guy. Next time I will squash him like a bug.

Or I emerge victorious, crushing my detractors. I am feared. I am powerful. That is, until the fear turns to anger and the anger becomes rebellion. I, like Caesar, have experienced backstabbing by my trusted colleagues, "Et tu, you guys?"

What if you could avoid the sniping, backstabbing, and call-to-arms in your workplace? What if there were no war? No skirmish? No problem?

Ego Gone Wild

My clients repeatedly vent about the slings and arrows of their outrageous torture at work. Whether teams or individuals, these workplace warriors express the desire for collaboration and cooperation to achieve their professional goals. The barrier to office harmony? An ego whose sole purpose is to defend and protect its take on reality.

Go back to where the war began. What did the back-hackers say about you?

You did not cross your T's!

And what was your reaction? "You're wrong!" is the war cry screamed by an ego attacked at its core belief.

How dare you? Of course, I crossed my T's. And correctly, too. I come from a long line of meticulous T-crossers.

Ego will find proof to support and protect itself.

Look at my white paper, my website, and the last six contracts I produced! All crossed! And i's dotted, too! In fact, I've noted serious error in your T crossings! And you have a big zit on your nose!

Ego goes to war

Without resistance, is there war? What if the ego hears a statement, and not an attack? What if the ego recognizes the statement as true? If ego recognizes truth, there is understanding. With understanding, there is no war.

Do the following exercises to awaken you to truth, the Truth about **you**.

Exercise 1: What I think and do.

Purpose: To grow eyes in the back of your head, in the front of your head, and inside your head. With a clear line of vision, you recognize the instrument of attack.

1. Create three columns. In column one, list all of the values that define your ethics and conduct: choose attributes such as punctuality, honesty, kindness, open-mindedness, and fairness.
2. In column 2, enter the opposite for each of the attributes.
3. In column three, briefly describe a time in your life – without judgment or shame – when you did not live up to the ideal in column one, and more closely lived out the attribute in column two.

   Your worksheet begins to look like to the example below, and might be as long as your arm!

1	2	3
Valued Attribute (I am or I want to be...)	**Opposite of the Attribute**	**EXAMPLE OF THE OPPOSITE**
Fair	Unfair	Gave the Acme account to John instead of Anne.
Punctual	Tardy	Late for my dental appointment last week.
Honest	Dishonest	Didn't return extra change to the store last week.

4. Read aloud what you have written, using the pattern below, to yourself or to a trusted friend.

- Being **(column 1)** is important to me. I was **(column 2)** when I **(column 3)**.

Example: Being <u>fair</u> is important to me. I was <u>unfair</u> when I <u>gave the Acme account to John instead of Anne.</u>

5. As you read each sentence, consider your example in column 3. Ask yourself:
   - Is it difficult to always live up to my own idealized expectations?
   - Is it possible that people at work noticed times when I haven't lived up to my own expectations?

By genuinely owning the part of you that isn't perfect and makes mistakes, critical comments from others begin to lose their edge. The blow is softer, shallower, and sometimes even misses the mark.

If a colleague says you are unfair, recognize that you have been unfair per your own observation. *You are unfair* loses its sharp edge, and you react less violently because you can find it in yourself. Your mind settled, you look at the situation as it is – someone judged you who isn't you – and you determine the next step from a vantage point of clear thinking.

Don't be too complacent. You have deflected this string of attacks, but you still have a big red target on your back.

Exercise 2: What they say.

Purpose: To identify attack strategies, and recognize your attacker.

a) Make a list of all of the dreadful, sniping, gossipy comments people say about you, write about you, or think about you. What do they say that bothers you? Use these statements to nudge your thinking as you create your list:

My boss says that I am...
My colleagues say that I am...
My subordinates, in talking with each other, say that I...
My clients say that I am...
I know they (boss, colleague, client, subordinates, cleaning crew, vendors) think I am...

b) Review your list. Next to each gripe, snipe, and comment note your mind's response to what *they* say.

c) Reread each statement, and take note of your physical reaction. Does your stomach immediately tighten up? Jaw clench? Toes curl? Briefly describe your reaction next to each statement. Your list will begin to look something like this:

[What they say] **She just sits in her office doing nothing.** [Your response] *How dare they? I work harder than anyone around here!* [Physical reaction] Bite my lip. Stomach churns. Where are the TUMS?

Don't you think he could get here on time for once? *I am always on time. Nobody seems to notice when Janie is always late.* Teeth grind. Shoulders tense.

You can't trust her. *How can they say that? Idiots. After all I've done for them.* Hands shake. Jaw tightens. Stomach churns. Where are the damn TUMS?

He is a jerk. *This is the thanks I get for taking the heat from the boss for their incompetence.* Head shakes. Lips are tight. Stomach on fire.

What do you react to? Does your body go into overdrive because of what they said, or because of what **you think** about their statement?

He is a jerk is a simple sentence. When I attach my *This is the thanks I get for taking the heat from the boss for their incompetence* thinking to the statement, I create the environment that causes the head shakes, the tight lips, and the bonfire in the pit of my stomach. The original concept doesn't create the pain in my... er... back; my thinking wrapped around the other's comment is the source of the pain. My thinking creates my stress, my anger, my ulcer.

What happens when you recognize that the knives in your back – in your stomach, in your jaw, in your head – are only a sampling of the increasingly large arsenal of weapons manufactured in your own mind? What happens when you recognize that you are your own attacker?

You put down your weapons and call a truce – with **you**.

Ego Sentry

Coach, after these exercises I feel bruised and battered. And besides that, I can clearly see my own fingerprints on the weapons! What is going on here?

And they pay me for this? You bet. They pay me to show them how to stop the war.

The ego protects itself by desperately holding on to its fundamental beliefs. Loosening the grip of those beliefs poses a threat to an individual's entire identity. A violent attack on the ego invites unrestrained resistance. Investigating the ego to discover truth requires a new tactic – diplomacy in uncovering what is actually true.

Through a simple, powerful process of inquiry into stressful thoughts she calls The Work, Byron Katie offers a basic template of four questions and turnarounds to dramatically shift beliefs around personal and business relationships. Leading edge corporations embrace Byron Katie's process of inquiry to assist their employees in developing a deeper understanding of the root of stress. Once understood, business stressors can be addressed with a clear mind that is innovative, creative, and open.

You either believe what you think or you question it. There's no other choice.

– Byron Katie

What are you thinking? The first step in inquiry is to recognize a stressful, painful, or otherwise disturbing thought. Choose an example from your list in Exercise 2, and ask yourself, "What am I thinking?"

Example: *I work harder than anyone around here.*

Is this thought true? (Yes or No)
Yes.

Are you sure? Is it absolutely true? Do you actually always work harder than anyone in your group, department, or organization? (Yes or No)

I guess I don't really know if the people downstairs work more than I do. No, I don't know.

What do you do, say, or feel when you believe that thought you are thinking?

I get angry and can't think or speak. If I speak I get tongue tied and look stupid. I get resentful and either sit at work and steam, or I simply go home because I don't want to work while everyone else is home with their family. I don't really get anything done.

What would you do if you couldn't think that thought? Who would you be without the thought *I work harder than anyone around here?*

I would just work until I got as much work finished as I wanted to and wouldn't worry whether other people are staying late or not. I wouldn't care if anyone saw me at work or not. I would be a better employee, and happier when I went home.

Turn it around. Our minds see things backwards – like a mirror image. Look at the opposite to see if you can find truth. Each opposite is called a **turnaround**. Give 3 examples of what makes each turnaround true for you.

Original: *I **work harder** than anyone around here.*
Turnaround 1: *I **do not work harder** than anyone around here.*

> Example 1: *I see some cars on the parking lot when I am here.*
> Example 2: *A few people get here before me in the morning.*
> Example 3: *I was off work for 2 weeks with my back problems.*

Turnaround 2: *I **work softer** than anyone around here.*

> Example 1: *I always travel first class... pretty soft!... and no one else does.*
> Example 2: *I have the best chair here because of my back problems – soft.*
> Example 3: *When I am here alone, I turn on my CD player and enjoy the music.*

Inquire into your stressful thoughts, and notice that the battle within quiets. What do you experience as you find the turnarounds? How might you manage your work differently – manage your life differently – as you recognize the truth in your turnarounds?

Example of living according to the truth you discovered in your turnarounds:
- *Notice who is working late when I am – maybe buy a pizza so we can have a break.*
- *It never occurred to me to recognize the people who get there early – I don't even really know how early they come in. I can ask. Maybe I will pick up some dough-nuts or bagels for them in the morning.*
- *Perhaps I will go to work earlier and not stay so late in the evening.*
- *I really do have a nice chair and notice that a few people don't have an ergonomic office space. I wonder if there is something that can be done about that.*
- *I can get an mp3 player and listen to music all day at work without disturbing anyone. I'm less likely to be distracted, and I find it soothing.*

Notice the room in your thinking for constructive approaches to your work environment and colleagues because – at least for now – you have calmed the warrior in you. You have declared a truce in the real battleground, your thinking.

When you walk away from the war, there is no one left to fight. Snipers and back-hackers have no weapon, no target – and you don't attack them. Peace in your mind. Peace in your office environment. (Go to www.thework.com for more information on The Work of Byron Katie.)

Shifting to Peaceful Communication

But Coach, what about the other guys? Even if I completely change, and never have another stressful thought, what do I do about them – the other people at work? Even if we disarm the slings and arrows of anger and distrust, how do we communicate effectively to discourage backbiting, backstabbing, and groin injuries?

Know thyself.   Once you are clear regarding real or imagined transgressions, deficiencies, accusations, and injustices you will notice a change in the people around you. Subtle or dramatic, there will be a noticeable shift in their behavior. (And do not trust me on that. Try it out for yourself; I would love to hear your story via email at <u>dee@ toplevelcoach.com</u>)

Respond graciously to compliments and other nice stuff. Do you *except* or *accept* expressions of appreciation or gratitude from your colleagues?

> Wayne: *Wow, Molly, great job getting that TSP report put together – and so professionally! – in such short order. You are amazing.*
>
> Molly: *Oh, no problem. It wasn't such a big deal. It is just part of my job-duh. You don't need to thank me.*

In this self-deprecating exchange, Molly teaches Wayne to ignore Molly's efforts, and to be more critical in determining what constitutes an achievement that actually deserves recognition. By cutting off Wayne's honest communication of appreciation, Molly effectively sabotaged communication around high-stress issues. Molly got it done efficiently *except* it was no problem, *except* it wasn't a big deal, *except* it was just part of her job. And by the way, it is a colossal waste of time thanking her.

> Mike: *Hey, Bethany, you rock! I can't believe how quickly you arranged Myron's move to the basement. You are a genius.*
>
> Bethany: *Thank you. It means a lot to me that you noticed.*

Bethany heard Mike, and recognized his appreciation of a job well done. She acknowledged the value of her contribution, and further expanded the level of communication with Mike. Bethany *accepted* his thanks as a gift, and opened or reinforced a channel of communication with Mike.

When is *accept*ance difficult for you? Notice your reaction to the following:

Compliment	Communication Corker
You are smart.	I could be smarter.
You did a good job.	It wasn't a big deal.
Your desk is cleaner than mine.	You should have seen it yesterday.
You are so lucky!	Not really. I've had plenty of problems.
How do you always remember everything?	I don't. I just called my son "Peppi" this morning. That's my dog.
I wish everyone liked me the way they like you.	Believe me, I have plenty of enemies.

Be mindful in your communication and encourage honest exchanges; offer genuine praise and appreciation. Learn *accept*ance. Respond to a compliment with a "Thank you." End of story.

If You Don't Have Anything Nice to Say...

I've heard it before. No one wants to tell anyone anything *negative*. They want to be nice and *positive*.

I'm positive *that guy just screwed up the project.*
I'm positive *the testing was done with flawed*
equipment.
I'm positive *Donna doesn't know how to make a chart.*

Not positive in a *positive* sense, of course. Usually uttered first to co-workers (amassing the troops!), these statements are the first rumblings of attack.

Did you ever observe another's behavior and recognize an opportunity for improvement? Yes, it is likely you have. Did you say something to the responsible individual, the person who could benefit from your observation? Not likely. The inability to deliver honest feedback is the primary cause of destructive organizational gossip and sniping. Feedback on performance becomes an accusation. "I can't believe Sam screwed up the schedule like that. Now everyone has to work overtime to make up the time. Doesn't he know what this does to the rest of us? Doesn't he know how to put together a schedule?"

In my work with project and department managers, I regularly see critical statements circulated throughout a team like a perverse game of *telephone*. The one person always excluded from the game – and kept in the dark by some twisted sense of kindness by her teammates – is the target of the criticism. By the time management hears the story, the remedy to the situation has reached a level of complexity that becomes a project in itself. Result: Rapidly deteriorating morale, a ruined reputation, and wasted time and resources.

Responsible, resourceful managers create a productive environment for those under their direction. These savvy managers enlist my assistance in the ceasefire, and in

building the atmosphere of trust and cooperation necessary for ongoing collaboration.

But Coach, I am just one person in a toxic environment of
blame, shame, and body odor. What can I do?

Exercise 3: The 3 things I [blank] about you.

**Purpose: To clearly see your enemy, and confront your
own terrorist attack instruments – your thoughts.**

a) On a sheet of paper, write down the name of a co-
   worker that you avoid on team projects or in your
   daily tasks. Example: **Billy Crabbon**
b) Identify three things that you dislike [hate, despise,
   detest] about working with Billy.
   - He wears so much cologne that it makes my stom-
     ach turn and gives me a headache.
   - He worries about every little detail including the
     color pen I sign approvals with. He is crazy! Who
     worries about that stuff anyway?
   - He never comes in to work on the weekends like
     everyone else when we are on a tight deadline.
     He's not a team player!
c) Remove the emotion and everything but "the facts"
   from the statements in (b).
   - He wears cologne. I get nauseous. I get a head-
     ache.
   - He pays attention to details.
   - He doesn't work weekends.
d) Identify three things you like or admire about Billy.
   - He has a picture of his little girls and wife on his
     desk.

- I saw him bring in doughnuts one Friday, and he didn't tell anyone they were from him. He let one of the other guys take the credit.
- Speaking of taking credit, we brainstormed ideas once and he gave me all of the credit for the solution.

Notice the progression of thought: a) Identify a target; b) React emotionally; c) Distill the facts; d) Humanize and personalize.

Identify clearly the issue at hand, and you begin to recognize the humanness of your co-worker. With this discovery, you naturally begin the shift to peaceful communication in your workplace and in your life. You discover your sphere of control – **you**.

... Then Say It.

Coach, this is great. I feel good about myself, my co-worker, and the world. Peaceful. And tomorrow I have a meeting with Billy and my nostrils are already twitching and I've stockpiled Excedrin. I don't see the relief here.

The next step is to apply your personal power, and experience your release from the prison you have constructed in your mind. You are going to ask for exactly what you want. No judgment. No shame. No fear.

Go back to the statements in (b) above.
- *He wears cologne. I get nauseous. I get a headache.*
- *He pays attention to details.*
- *He doesn't work weekends.*

Go directly to Billy. (Do not pass Go. Do not stop at the Boss, the Best Buddy, or the Receptionist's candy dish.) Kindly and fearlessly address your three areas of concern to Billy.

> *Billy, I have a few things to share with you [discuss with you/ask you]. Is this a good time for you?*

If Billy says *No*, ask for a time that would be more convenient, and schedule a time. If Billy says *Yes*, use the statements from (b) above to formulate your questions. First, state your observation of the facts. Secondly, ask for what you want. Be specific.

- [Observation] *Billy, I notice that when I smell your cologne I get a headache and a little nauseous.* [What I want] *It would be helpful to me if you didn't wear it.*
- *Billy, it seems that you have a sharp eye for detail. You recently noticed that I signed the document in black pen, and mentioned I needed a blue one. Could you please explain the reasoning behind that?*
- *Billy, we are working most weekends to meet the project deadline, and are less productive when you aren't here to answer questions. Do you have some ideas on how we can overcome that barrier on the weekends?*

You never know what Billy will say. Below are two possible responses.

Billy's Response A: *Are you kidding me? People pick on me all the time about that cologne. Fine. I won't wear it. Are you telling me you haven't been trained in approvals? You've been here longer than me, so I find that hard to believe. Talk to Steve about it. I don't work weekends. Period.*

If this response angers, frustrates, or sends you running for the candy machine, start by telling Billy "Thank you for your time." Go back to Exercise 3 and distill the facts from the emotion:
- Billy said he won't wear the cologne,
- you should speak to Steve, and
- he (Billy) won't work weekends.

Your next steps are clear: Speak to Steve, and discuss with your manager how to overcome the issue of Billy not working weekends when timelines are tight. Good to know that Billy won't be wearing that cologne any more! Repeat Exercise 3 until you get what you want – an answer to the blue pen issue, and an efficient way to work around Billy's weekend absences.

Billy's Response B: *I'm not too crazy about that cologne either. My mother gave it to me. I'm sorry it caused a problem for you and I'm glad you told me. Of course I won't wear it to work any more. The blue pen is a quality rule. It makes it easier for document control to find the original signatures. I thought everybody knew that. And I would like to come in on weekends, but my wife takes care of her mom and I watch our kids. Her mom has Alzheimer's and when my wife stays with her mom – it is the only break her dad gets all week. You know, I could take phone calls or IM to answer questions – as long as everyone understands that I might be just a little delayed in answering if my kids need something.*

Clear, honest communication gives rise to clear, honest responses. When the war stops and you recognize your colleagues and partners – and not enemy commandos – alliances grow. Synergies develop that propel personal and organizational performance beyond old war-torn territories. You become a beacon of openness, creativity, and innovation.

You write the treaty. You end the war. The peace is where it has always been and can only be – in **you**.

Agree to Agree – with You

Coach, these are great exercises and I see their value in defusing explosive situations in the office. It occurs to me that it might take awhile for me to learn to integrate all of this into my daily routine. And there are other issues at work you haven't even discussed: email-snipers, nepotism, unreasonable expectations, budget tightening, power-hungry despots, and jelly doughnuts!

In my coaching practice I use many strategies to shift the office paradigm to peaceful communication. Each workplace is unique in its culture, issues, and battle scars. These powerful exercises apply universally to any toxic environment – home, office, Christmas at Aunt Charlotte's – and can be used by both individuals and groups. As Coach, I become a kind of superconductor for positive change in the workplace. Working with management and staff, I uncover the landmines, bayonets, and the Weapons of Mass Morale Destruction throughout the organization. Together we dismantle the armament and set free the collaboration, creativity, and productivity within each individual employee. (For more information and additional worksheets, go to www.toplevelcoach.com.)

Be patient with yourself, and notice the effect that each averted battle has on your daily attitude and productivity. I invite you to declare a Four-Day Truce with your boss, your co-workers, your clients, your vendors, and the soup server in the lunch line.

Your Four-Day Truce. Choose four consecutive days during your work week, e.g. Monday through Thursday, Tuesday through Friday.

A. On the morning of the first day of the challenge, rate each of the last four business days on a scale of 1-10 (1=Horrid, 10=Fabulous). Add the four ratings together, and file your ratings and your total in a safe place.
B. Practice exercises 1-3 each day. At the end of each day, rate that day on a scale of 1-10 (1=Horrid, 10=Fabulous).
C. At the end of the fourth day, write down your observations. Some examples:
   • *People laughed at me when I...*
   • *John actually said my idea was a good one. This is a first!*
   • *I felt silly when Bill thanked me and I said "You're welcome." It felt good, too.*
   • *I told John I needed his report today because the customers will be here in the morning. He actually delivered it and seemed pleased when I thanked him. He even asked if I needed anything else!*
D. The morning of day five, add the ratings for the four days of your Truce. Subtract your Truce Rating from your Pre-Truce Rating (from A above). The difference is your overall experience of improvement in your workplace during the Truce.

Numerical results vary among my clients. While some clients experience a five-point improvement over four days, others experience a positive change of more than sixteen points. The numbers themselves aren't important; the reduced stress and improved productivity is.

You determine if or how you will use these skills at the end of your four days. You may find that these exercises become a daily practice. You may notice that you employ these tools only under certain extraordinary circumstances. Whatever the decision, you have a model for daily work in a peace paradigm.

Deflect snipers, landmines, and covert attacks of every type with clear motives, clear communication, and clear thinking. As you work through the exercises in this chapter, be mindful of the following simple guidelines inspired by Don Miguel Ruiz' Four Agreements to repel the slings and arrows in your workplace:

1. Adhere to a high standard of professional integrity.
2. What other people think of you is none of your business. Respect yourself.
3. Be clear and concise in your communication.
4. Do the best you know how to do, and appreciate that others do the best they know how to do. Seek help when you need it.

In the End. You have options. Really.
- You can do what you have always done.
- You can escape.
- You can better your environment, and build a space that offers you satisfaction, collaboration and creativity.

And each and every day **you** make the choice to fuel the war, or to end it – at the office and in your life.

૱

Special thanks to dear Miriam, who taught me respite.

Dee Carrell is a certified coach and professional business consultant who understands the challenges you face at work. She bases her coaching on leading edge techniques designed to uncover and eliminate needless fears that keep you from achieving your true potential for personal and professional success. For more information on moving to the next level in your career - and in life - visit Dee at www.TopLevelCoach.com.

CB

Finally Write That Book!

by Anna Paradox

I'm in a particularly good position to hear about books people want to write. I help writers write. So, just about every time I mention my work and there's a dozen people in the room, someone comes up to tell me about this book they've always wanted to write. You know what? Most of the time, these books have the potential to be very fine books. I'm gathering quite a bit of evidence for the idea that everyone contains a book.

Here's a secret: most of these books will never be written.

People want to write books for a lot of reasons. Sometimes they hope to become the next Stephen King or J. K. Rowling and make a lot of money. Sometimes they simply want to tell their story. They may want to help other people by sharing what they've learned. Others seek the respect of being an author – and let me tell you, I have seen these aspiring authors multiply their self-respect by finishing a book. Some want to boost their business by putting their expertise in print – and that works too. Sometimes there is a story that lodges in their hearts and keeps whispering "Tell me."

Some of these reasons are more likely to come true than others. Only one person in six billion is Stephen King – his name is Stephen King. His particular combination of talent, persistence, and suiting the desires of his readers has created his success. Still, watching myself and other writers, I have become convinced that writing is never wasted.

Writing is discovery – both of yourself and your subject. As the words go onto the paper, you learn about yourself – yes, you can do this. Yes, these are the words that carry this thought to someone else. Yes, this is what you know. You also own what you write about at a deeper level when you've captured the words that express it.

Authors are experts – they have to be. A solid book holds more information than a full day seminar. A textbook can hold the knowledge in an entire semester of a college course. By the time all those words fill the pages, the author needs to know enough to write them. In our society, experts receive better pay – and they deserve it. Writing a book will both make you an expert and – just as importantly for business – let people see that you are an expert.

And writing a book can fulfill a deeply human need to connect with other people. It gives the author a spacious canvas to express dreams, desires, experiences, and wisdom. It starts a conversation that can continue beyond the author's life.

Let's say that for one of these reasons – or for a reason entirely your own – you want to write a book. Let me also guess that you're reading this because you haven't yet written that book. Now what?

Why Many Books Will Never Be Written

First of all, a book can be a dauntingly large project. There's all that effort of becoming an expert – even if only an expert on the landscape of your novel or the story of your own life. There's putting those words on the page, one after another – whoa, one hundred thousand words really sounds like a lot! Then there's the mysterious world of publishing and marketing your book. So much new territory and so many details – can you climb that mountain?

Then, there's the question of time. Where do you find the time to write a book? You've been going along, filling all the hours of your days, while not writing a book. Is it worth trading some of those activities for writing?

And finally, there's the fact that writing can be just plain unpleasant. The idea of having written appeals to many people a lot more than the process of writing. I have some theories about that – and some useful tools to make writing more enjoyable. Writers come to me, and together we solve these problems and more. In this chapter, I'll show you some methods for overcoming these hurdles right now.

These three reasons not to write tend to reinforce each other. We'll take them one at a time – because that is how to solve them.

How to Deal with an Overwhelming Project

"How do you eat an elephant? One bite at a time."

Yes, a book is like an elephant – at least in the sense that it needs to be broken down into small pieces. It's not so much like an elephant in the sense that it weighs two tons and eats two hundred pounds of roughage every day. Although it may feel like it.

Let's look at breaking a book into small pieces. One convenient piece of a book is one page. I first encountered the one page a day plan in Lawrence Block's excellent book *Telling Lies for Fun and Profit*. One page is much more approachable than a book. One page a day for one year yields 365 pages – a substantial book. Take Sundays off, and you'll still complete 300 pages. One book a year makes a respectable writing career. One book every two or three years? Still a solid production.

In terms of words per day, two hundred and fifty words also leads to a substantial book in a year. We speak English at between one hundred to two hundred words a minute. If your goal is to be Lionel Fanthorpe – who once wrote eighty-nine books in three years – you could dictate fifty thousand words in a weekend, and have a short book. Maybe you'd prefer to think a bit, slow down to one-tenth the pace of speaking, and write only ten words a minute. That's two hundred and fifty words in about half an hour. You'd easily reach a moderate seventy-five thousand word book in a year. Even an epic two hundred thousand word tome could be complete in less than three years.

Slow and steady really does win the race – especially when it comes to long term projects. That's why my teacher Martha Beck calls breaking a task into small pieces "turtle steps." And here's another secret I learned from her – if even fifteen minutes a day sounds like too much, make it less. Divide your starting task into smaller pieces until it's shrug-your-shoulders, do-it-now simple. Start there. Five minutes a day? One word? Go for it! You can always increase it as you go. Try adding one minute or one word every four days.

And if that's what you needed to start writing, by all means, go write now! I'll be around when you want more.

How to Find the Time to Write

Now that you know the time to write could be as little as five minutes a day, maybe you already know how to grab that time for yourself. Excellent!

Or, you may still feel scheduled minute by minute with very important tasks. Also excellent!

Truly, if your entire life is filled with gratifying, productive, enjoyable, and contributing activities, I am glad for you. You display a very rare ability to make the most of your time. Your days pass in a joyful, successful series of accomplishments, and you are probably supporting your family and your community while pulling down a six-figure income. Wow, you rock. Wait – why are you reading this chapter?

By far the more common situation among the aspiring authors I've encountered is that they reach the end of the day and go, "Oops, I meant to write. What happened to the day?" More generally, I hear that they don't have time to write – but they still want to.

I believe in listening to that little voice that says you want to write. (We'll talk about some other voices that I believe in shoving into a concrete block and pushing off the end of the pier later.) That voice is there because writing offers you something you aren't getting now. If you have the desire to write, you deserve the time to write.

It doesn't take long. Practice being unfussy about your writing time. How quickly can you go from your other tasks to writing? Can you grab a notebook and pen and start writing, wherever, whenever? Can you turn on the computer, and open up your document and write, do not pass email, do not check the latest frog racing website? If you do need a transition to writing, how much do you need? Would ten conscious breaths do it? Or brewing a cup of tea?

Buy a timer. Find out exactly how long it takes you to prepare to write. You can also use the timer to count down your five to fifteen minute writing session.

Let's say your total time for preparing to write and actually writing is fifteen minutes. You've tested it, you've timed it, and you want to do it. And yet you still don't know when you can take fifteen minutes to write.

What's your next step? Fill out this handy dandy worksheet!

Worksheet

How Do I Use My Time?

From midnight to one a.m., I did this:

From one to two a.m., I did this:

From two to three a.m., I did this:

From three to four a.m., I did this:

From four to five a.m., I did this:

From five to six a.m., I did this:

From six to seven a.m., I did this:

From seven to eight a.m., I did this:

From eight to nine a.m., I did this:

From nine to ten a.m., I did this:

From ten to eleven a.m., I did this:

From eleven to noon, I did this:

From noon to one p.m., I did this:

From one to two p.m., I did this:

From two to three p.m., I did this:

From three to four p.m., I did this:

From four to five p.m., I did this:

From five to six p.m., I did this:

From six to seven p.m., I did this:

From seven to eight p.m., I did this:

From eight to nine p.m., I did this:

From nine to ten p.m., I did this:

From ten to eleven p.m., I did this:

From eleven to midnight, I did this:

I don't know which hours you sleep, or when you eat, or what time your appointment with the governor is, so I've put in all 24 hours. Make several copies (with my happy permission) and for the next three days, write down how you spent your day, all day long, in one hour intervals.

Then go through each hour, and ask yourself, "Is this more important to me than writing? Is it more fun?" See if you find one portion of an hour each day that you'd rather spend on writing.

You can even take it a step further, by breaking some of your hours into fifteen minute intervals. Want to jot down what you are doing every fifteen minutes all day long? Go for it!

What if you find that you have to do everything you are doing? I encourage you to investigate that thought through The Work of Byron Katie, available at www.thework.com.

Really look at that list of your daily activities. Especially examine the ones that feel heavy and unpleasant. If you spend time in ways that give you no joy, consider this list of alternatives, astutely alliterated by Martha Beck: Bag it, Barter it, Better it, or Behold it. Bag it – just don't do it. Barter it – find someone else to do it, in trade for money or services. Better it – improve your working conditions. Behold it – truly look at it with deep awareness. One way to make your life better and better is to continuously weed out the parts you like least. I love to edit – others would rather pull teeth. So let them! With six billion people on this planet, there is bound to be someone who would take more pleasure in doing those tasks you dread than you do.

If you want to write, there is something on that list that can make room for writing. If writing is one of the tasks you dread – take a look at the next section.

When Writing is Unpleasant

Do you know how sometimes you don't notice what's right in front of you until someone else points it out? That's how I felt one day when a friend observed that the most self-critical people she knew were writers. Of course they are! I've seen that all my life! How did I miss it?!

Since then, I've confirmed the trend. I've taken informal surveys of writers and non-writers, and sure enough, the writers tend to dissect themselves and their work more harshly than the non-writers.

I have a couple theories about that. My first theory is that writing is observation. A writer looks at the world, and translates it into words. That observation can spill over onto the writer's self – and it's all too easy to pay more attention to what's wrong than what's right.

The second theory is that the part of the brain that composes words is very close to the part of the brain that holds that critical inner voice. So, writing brings out the inner critic. Ouch!

I have no proof for either of these theories. They just suit what I've seen of my own mind and heard from other writers. We often dread writing, and not because it's physically uncomfortable. We dread it because of how we feel when we write.

Just look at these typical thoughts about writing:

> I'm a bad writer.
> This isn't good enough.
> I don't know what to say.
> I don't have anything worth saying.
> That sentence sucks!
> No one wants to read this.
> I'll never sell anything.
> What's the use, it won't get published.
> Yeah, that paragraph makes sense,
>   lamebrain.
> I don't know enough to write.
> This isn't working.
> Who am I to write?

No wonder we hate writing! I feel depressed just reading that list.

Thoughts like these are a completely unnecessary burden on the writing process. Think a thought like one of those, and writing becomes unpleasant! Who would want to find time to sit around insulting yourself?

Well, not me. Fortunately, even though writers have a talent for it, I have discovered that self-criticism is not necessary to the writing process. In fact, once I learned to turn down the volume on the inner critic, I started writing faster and more often, and having a lot more fun. The inner criticism steals the energy a writer needs to be creative. By letting go of judgments about the writing (or delaying them until the editing process), a writer receives a better flow of words and ideas. This has worked for my clients, too. All you need are some tools for changing your thoughts.

There are a lot of tools available! Spiritual leaders and philosophers have been studying how to change thoughts for thousands of years. Various styles of meditation combine discipline and awareness into practices to gain control of thought. Silent prayer is directed thought. In the twentieth century, we had entire schools of people studying positive thought. Oh, yes, the technology is out there.

So, if you have a technology that's working for you, by all means, apply it to your thoughts about writing.

If you don't, let me save you sorting through the options and recommend two outstanding resources.

The first is The Work of Byron Katie. There's a reason so many of us coaches refer clients to this tool. It's extremely potent. These four questions free anyone who authentically seeks the truth through them. They are best approached in a gentle, seeking, meditative way. Kindly look inside as you ask each question to discover what is true for you. Writers may find pen and journal an especially nourishing method to explore the questions.

The second is EFT, a tapping exercise thoroughly documented at www.emofree.com. I like this one because it is physical – it gives me a break from all the words. I've had very good results with this. It's fast and simple, taking well less than two minutes. The first step is to focus on a problem, and the second step is to tap a short sequence of particular points on the face, chest, and hands.

Oh, what the heck, here's one more. Brooke Castillo has written a short, friendly guide that pulls together the essentials of at least eight different teachers. Have a look at *Self Coaching 101*. She gives great worksheets for changing any negative result into a better one by changing your thoughts. Her book is a great starting point for investigating those other teachers, too.

Consider the time you spend improving your thoughts an investment. It will pay off by making your writing time much more pleasant and productive.

I've heard rumors it improves the rest of your life, too.

Putting it All Together

I love writing. I love what writing a book can do for people. A book can improve your business, offer companionship to distant friends, and be a legacy. More than that, the journey of writing a book transforms the writer into a greater person. By writing, we discover more about ourselves and the world, and we share those discoveries. I truly believe that writing a book is a noble pursuit.

I love helping writers write, too. It's my very great privilege to have supported my clients to finding their authentic voices, taking joy in writing, and sending their words to their readers. Their experiences have improved what I have to give you.

They have made my tools better, including the ones in this chapter for three very common reasons that people don't write books, even when they want to. Notice how these challenges fit together. When all three problems are in play, a book becomes an overwhelming, dreaded burden, impossible to fit into your schedule. On the other hand, solve one of those problems, and the other two become smaller. By taking it one small step at a time, it's easier to find the time to write. And when writing is more fun, it's much more appealing to find the time and take those small steps.

If you are an aspiring author, you can write that book. You can even enjoy writing it. Honor that desire and start taking steps to complete your book right away.

☙

With thanks to my clients – it's my joy to see your words bloom – and to Doug Weathers, for twenty-three years of married bliss and counting.

Anna Paradox is a writing coach. She's dedicated to helping writers enjoy bringing their authentic voice to readers. Her coaching improves both the experience of writing and its output. This marks the fourth published book to credit her as editor. She offers a free e-course called Great Writers on Great Ideas at www.BridgeOfWords.com, and you can contact her at anna@annaparadox.com.

Please see bibliography on p. 257.

☙

Practical Guide to Making Good Choices

by Alina Bas

Did you ever go through an internal struggle of Biblical proportions when making a choice? Some choices are made naturally. Others have the potential to put us through agony that can last for hours, days, and even years, sometimes lingering long after a choice is made. Our decisions can range from the seemingly trivial ones – such as whether to take the stairs or the elevator – to significant ones, like whether to take out a mortgage in the current economy. How do we make good choices consistently? What makes a *good choice*?

This chapter offers a systematic way of *making choices that make sense to you* and with which you can live in peace. Let's define a *good choice* as a choice that meets the following two criteria:

- It brings you closer to whatever it is that you want to accomplish in life
  AND
- Regardless of the outcome, looking back at your choice you will always know that you made the best possible decision at the given time.

Based on my education, research and experience, I developed a systematic five-step approach to consistently making good choices:

Step 1. Clarify the Goal That You Want To Accomplish By Making a Choice
Step 2. Define Your Options
Step 3. Use Logic
Step 4. Listen to Your Intuition
Step 5. Get To Know Your Inner Community

This five-step approach is not best for decisions that need to be made on the spot because it takes time. The five steps are most helpful when making choices that feel consequential to you. For example, it may not be worth your time to use all of the steps if you are determining whether to watch "American Idol" or "Dancing with the Stars." It will be useful, though, when deciding whether to accept a job offer in Denver or stay put in New York City. Also, if you find yourself unable to make a decision and you are not sure why, this systematic approach can help you understand and address hidden challenges. For example, an issue like having your intuition at odds with your logic would definitely surface as you go through the steps.

STEP 1. CLARIFY THE GOAL THAT YOU WANT TO ACCOMPLISH BY MAKING A CHOICE

The reason why we make choices is to accomplish certain goals. The right goals define the choices that we really face. Sometimes properly defining the goal can make the choice immediately obvious. For example, if you are deciding whether to move to Denver or stay put in New York

City, consider your motivation for making this choice. If your main goal is to live close to your parents, the problem may require one solution. If your main goal is to be in the city that offers the best career opportunities in your field, the problem may require a different approach. So, before making a choice, it is important to figure out what your *true* goal is.

A *true* goal is something that you truly desire, not something that you *should* desire. A true goal comes from the core of your being. One way to differentiate between a *should* goal and a *true* goal is to be honest with yourself. For example, if you say "My goal is to become a doctor," ask yourself: "*Is it true* that I want to become a doctor?" Explore your motivation. It may very well turn out that you truly want to heal people's ailments through the use of traditional medicine. It may also turn out that you want to help people by any means, which may be accomplished in many other ways than becoming a doctor. If it turns out that what you want is to get into a well-paid and well-respected occupation, it is a different goal than that of becoming a doctor. Whatever your goal may be, ask yourself: "Is it true?" and listen. Re-shape your goal until it rings absolutely true to you.

One of my clients (let's call her Sharon), wanted to start exercising. Yet she seemed unwilling or unable to make any steps towards it. Her original goal was: *I want to exercise every day.* Here is a summary of the way we worked through her goal:

Sharon: *I want to exercise every day.*
Coach: *Is it true?*
Sharon: *Of course! I just don't have the time.*
Coach: *Is it true that you don't have the time?*

Sharon: *Well, I can make the time, but I dread going to the gym.*
Coach: *Is it true that you dread going to the gym?*
Sharon: *Yes! It's an inconvenience to change into the gym clothes. It's also annoying to have to wait for the machines. I don't want to do it.*
Coach: *So, what would make your goal true?*
Sharon: *I want to exercise every day in a way that does not involve going to the gym and doesn't require changing into the workout clothes.*

Considering the fact that Sharon's original choice was whether to schedule an hour of gym time in the a.m. or in the p.m., I can confidently say that re-defining her goal saved her a great deal of time and aggravation. Once she found her true goal, Sharon quickly decided on brisk 30-minute walks during lunch hour to help her burn calories.

Let's do an exercise that will help you focus on your true goal. It is important that you work through the exercises *in writing.* Writing will help you clarify your ideas. It has been demonstrated that people who write down their New Year resolutions, for example, are more likely to accomplish their goals than people who do not write down their resolutions. So, please grab a pen or a pencil before you start the following exercise.

Exercise 1. Establishing My True Goal.

Think of a choice that you are currently facing. For example, moving or staying, breaking up or staying together, investing in a particular property or saving the money for a better deal. Write down the goal that you are trying to accomplish by making this decision: _____
_____

Ask yourself *honestly*: is your goal true? If not, which parts of your goal can you re-frame to make the goal true?

_____

_____

If you defined your goal at this point, I commend you. It is a big important step. Don't be discouraged if a clear goal still escapes you. It is a difficult task, so please allow yourself time and make it *a work in progress*.

CƷ

STEP 2. DEFINE YOUR OPTIONS

In addition to defining the decision to be made, a true goal also determines the options that you have. Your options may open up or disappear, depending on the way you define your goal.

Erica came to me determined to change jobs. She quickly outlined her options to me, and wanted my help determining the best choice among her options. Here is how we worked on her goal in order to understand her true options:

Erica's original goal:
> *Change jobs.*

Erica's original options:
> 1. *Give notice as soon as possible.*

2. *Take vacation time and use it to look for another job full-time.*
3. *Wait to secure another job and then give notice.*

After some soul-searching, Erica's story unraveled: "I like my job, but I can't stand the way my manager talks to me." Whenever you hear the word *but*, pay close attention: whatever comes after the *but* can give you a good idea about the way you really feel. (I really like you, *but...* I agree with you, *but...* This makes sense, *but....*)

Erica's true goal revealed:

Work with a manager who values and encourages my feedback.

Erica's true options:

1. *Find a more personable manager within the same company and transfer internally.*
2. *Find a way to work more effectively with the current manager.*
3. *Look for a different company with a supportive culture.*

The following exercise can help you define options that you have when facing your choice.

Exercise 2: Options That Support My True Goal.

Think about a specific decision that you need to make. If possible, use an example that will have significant consequences in your life: _____
_____
_____

Consider the reason why you are making this decision. What is your goal (i.e. what are you hoping to accomplish by making the decision)? _____
_____

Do a quick reality check: is your goal really true? Below please list options that can help you accomplish your goal. Be as creative as you can, and don't edit yourself at this point:

1. _____
2. _____
3. _____
4. _____
5. _____
6. _____
7. _____
8. _____
9. _____
10. _____

For the time being, I am asking you not to judge your ideas. Simply write them down. Allow a possibility that each idea has a gift for you: it could be a gift of remembrance, desire, adventure, connection, or spontaneity. Rather than discard improbable options, ask yourself how you can make them happen. Ask yourself what gifts there may be for you in those options, regardless of whether or not the options are reasonable.

ೞ

STEP 3. USE LOGIC

If you are an analytical person, you probably make lists of pros and cons every time you face an important decision. If you tend to make decisions based on your heart's desires rather than logical analysis, you will find that the next exercise provides an easy and useful way of capturing your mind's perspective.

Exercise 3: Using Logic to Evaluate Options

Pick three options from Exercise 2 that appeal to you most based on your personal preference, availability of your resources, or any other criteria that makes sense to you.

Option 1:

_____

In the PROS column, write down all the reasons why this is potentially a good option. In the CONS column, write the reasons why the option above is potentially a bad one. Please don't put anything in the SCORE columns yet.

PROS	SCORE	CONS	SCORE
_____	____	_____	____
_____	____	_____	____
_____	____	_____	____
_____	____	_____	____
_____	____	_____	____
_____	____	_____	____
_____	____	_____	____
_____	____	_____	____
_____	____	_____	____

TOTAL: _____   TOTAL: _____

Now please go back to each pro and con, and assign a weight to each. The scale is from 1 to 10, with 1 being <u>unim</u>portant in terms of making an impact on your life, and 10 being <u>very</u> important and having potential to affect your life significantly. After all the scores are assigned, please tally up the scores for each column.

Use a separate piece of paper to go through this exercise for each of your other options. It is likely that one of your options will have a higher score in the PROS column than others, which will tell you that logically it is your best option.

₧

So, your scores are calculated, and the choice is made, right? Not exactly. The next step is to figure out how you *feel* about your scores. In November of 2008, Radio Lab (an NPR program) aired an episode about a man who lost his ability to experience emotions as a result of having a brain tumor removed. When faced with a choice, he did not have an emotional response to the options when making decisions. Instead, he had to rely purely on a logical analysis. Things like choosing a cereal in the morning became cumbersome: it could take hours to analyze the pros and cons of choosing a cereal, evaluating the content for sugar, carbs, fiber, vitamins, and more. Having to choose from more than two options had a potential to complicate the choice significantly. In this man's case, *having a feeling* about the cereals would have facilitated his decision. Having a feeling about each of your options and taking those feelings into consideration can help you make a good choice. In the next section of the chapter, let's talk about feelings. Specifically, *how to listen to your gut,* and *how to tell whether or not your heart is into something.*

გკ

STEP 4. LISTEN TO YOUR INTUITION

My client Paula wanted to quit her job and start a business. We were working on finding a business that would work for her lifestyle and personality. One day, Paula started our session by saying: "I think I found a business that I am going to buy." In that instant, I got an image of a Victorian house. The work that was done in the house felt tranquil to me. There was a scent of candles and incense in the house. The house looked like it was situated away from the main road, and didn't get visitors from the street. My impression was that while the business in the house was well-established, it did not have a large enough client base to remain relevant, and that marketing for this business was nonexistent. This intuitive experience gave me a strong impression that the business was not the best match for Paula; it didn't have enough energy in it. How could all of this information have crossed my mind based on one phrase, "I think I found a business that I am going to buy"?

As Paula shared with me more information about this business, I learned that it was a family-run spa that was indeed operating way under capacity, out of a Victorian house. The business would have required a significant investment to help it grow. Paula decided against buying it. My intuitive assessment of the business turned out to be accurate. If I were an intuitive consultant rather than a life coach, I would have simply advised my client against buying the business. Instead, as a life coach I helped Paula explore whether she is willing to invest the necessary resources into this business. She decided that she was not. Paula had enough experience and resources to make this business work, but I think her intuition was telling her the same thing as mine: this was not the right business for her.

In our daily interactions, we make choices that appeal to us for one reason or another and those reasons are not always clear or logical. This is often described as *intuition*: a *hunch* or a *gut feeling*, a sensation in the pit of the stomach that encourages us to proceed or retreat. According to Wikipedia, intuition is "...an insight seemingly independent of previous experiences or empirical knowledge." Some equate intuition with instinct. Intuition has also being described as an extension of our other senses like sight, smell, touch, taste and hearing. I believe that *intuition is simply a heightened ability to perceive environmental cues that we are generally unable to access on a conscious level.*

One way to deconstruct intuition is by using a tool called the Body Compass, created by Martha Beck. The following exercise will help you understand how the body compass works. After the exercise we will work on practical applications of the body compass in your daily life.

Exercise 4: Establishing Your Body Compass.

Please recall a negative event that you have experienced at any point in your life. It could be an illness, a break-up, an accident, or a major disappointment. Imagine that this event is happening to you <u>right now</u>: look around you and see what you saw then, smell what you smelled then, recall who was around you, and feel the sensation of being at the age that you were at the time. Re-live this experience in the present, and notice how your body responds to the situation. What words come to mind to describe your physical state of being?

_____

_____

Make sure that your words are describing your physical experience rather than your intellectual experience. For example, "I feel gutted out," "My chest tightens," "I am light-headed," "I want to curl up in a ball" are descriptions of your physical state. Statements like "I feel sad," "I am angry," "I feel like I want to punch someone" are statements that come from your mind as it tries to analyze your body's reaction. (In this exercise, we are trying to separate your actual experience of something from your intellectualization of the experience. For example, a description of the actual experience sounds like this: "I am eating a marshmallow, and it is a little sweet, soft, not too chewy," and the intellectualized version of the experience sounds like this: "This is a good marshmallow.")

Give a label to the physical state that you experienced. The label can be anything that is meaningful to you, and that refers to this particular physical state: _____

_____

Thank you for being such a good sport! Now, look around you, notice where you are, notice how your body feels, and notice what is around you. You are no longer in that terrible day, you are in Today. Please put the score of **-10** next to the label that you wrote above. This signifies your lowest lows in terms of your physical reaction to an external event.

Let's shift gears. Please recall a positive event that you have experienced at any point in your life. Maybe it was the time when you received a meaningful gift, went on special trip, won a game, or brilliantly closed a deal. Imagine that this event is happening to you <u>right now</u>: look around you and see what you saw then, smell what you smelled then, recall who was around you, and feel the sensation of being at the age that you were at the time. Re-live this experience in the present, and notice how your body responds to the situation. What words come to mind to describe your physical state of being?

_____

_____

Make sure that your words are describing your physical experience, for example "I feel like I am floating," "I feel butterflies in my stomach," "I breathe deeply," "My heart is racing." If you are an analytical person, you may be tempted to write down things like "I feel excited," "I feel free." Try to describe what *excited* or *free* feels like to your body. Give a label to the physical state that you experienced. The label can be anything that is meaningful to you, and that refers to this particular physical state:

_____

Please put the score of **+10** next to the label that you wrote above. This signifies your highest highs in terms of your physical reaction to an event.

ः

The theory behind the body compass is that your body has a physical reaction to everyone and everything that you encounter in your life. This reaction registers somewhere between -10 and +10 on your scale, and you experience it before you have a chance to evaluate the encounter on a conscious level. It seems that your body knows your true likes and dislikes even when your mind may have a different agenda. You can tell yourself that you love your job, but if your body reacts to your job with a physical sensation of -8, imagine the amount of stress that your body is experiencing on a daily basis. Bringing into awareness your physical reaction to situations, places, and people is critical in evaluating your options as you make important choices.

The body compass can help you significantly improve your wellbeing during your daily activities. Let's say your goal is to have a calcium-rich diet in order to strengthen your bones. You open a refrigerator, see a yogurt, and your body responds with "Ugh, -8!", while your mind says: "Yogurt is good for me because it has calcium!" If you notice this disparity between your physical and intellectual reaction, you can look for other foods that address your true goal (i.e. getting calcium) and don't generate a low body compass score. Perhaps your body will respond with a "Yum, +3" to a banana, which is also a good source of calcium? Experiment with your options and listen to your body.

You may feel that you don't always have the luxury of making decisions based on your body compass, which is fine. Simply be aware of this information and keep it for your consideration in addition to all the other sources of information.

Exercise 5: Using My Body Compass For Making Choices

Think of a specific decision that you need to make. Consider as many options as possible to make a decision in a way that accomplishes your goal. You may use the same options that came up during your brainstorm for Exercise 2. Please list your options below in the left column:

1._____
2._____
3._____
4._____
5._____
6._____
7._____
8._____
9._____
10._____

On the right side, please assign a score between -10 and +10 based on your body's reaction to each option. Try to do it quickly, without analyzing the option or the score. Simply note the physical sensation that you experience as each option is presented to you. Please do not read the assignment further until you complete the scoring.

Now that you have the body compass scores, think about the possible reasons why certain options appeal to you on the physical level more than others. Consider ways to modify each option in order to elicit a higher score.

ぐ

As homework for this chapter, put your body compass to use for a day. Experiment with it, play with it, notice your physical reaction to people around you, notice your reaction to each space that you enter, and to each item on your plate. This will give you a measure for the harmony or disparity between your analytical self (i.e. what you *think* you experience) and your physical self (i.e. what you *physically* experience).

ぐ

Intuition does not always express itself as a physical sensation. Intuitive impressions can also come as images, fleeting memories, unexpected resemblances or déjà vu. Intuition may be triggered by environmental factors of which we are not aware on the conscious level.

When I had to set up a new office, a colleague of mine suggested that I should use my intuition to recommend what would be the best placement of furniture in the office. He also challenged me that for each of my intuitive suggestions, he would find a reasonable explanation justified by the environment. I took on the challenge, pointing out exactly where I would put the desks, the book cases, the filing cabinets, and other furniture. When he asked me for the reasons why I selected these placements, I had no logical explanation. So, he walked through the office, measured it, looked at all the alcoves, corners, light fixtures and concluded: "You recommended putting the desks here because these two places have excellent overhead lighting, and that corner doesn't. You recommended putting the board on this wall so that when there are visitors, the information on the boards would not be immediately visible to them." In this logical manner, he explained each of my suggestions. The truth is that he was absolutely right. Except that I had honestly not considered any of those factors when making my recommendations.

I have not seen on the market an objective consistent model for explaining, measuring, or teaching intuition. So what I recommend is for you to find your own way to define your intuition. Observe it and document the information that your intuition gives you. You can do so by simply starting to keep track of your intuitive predictions about people, things and situations in your life. Over time, as events play out, you can juxtapose your intuitive information with the information of actual events and see whether there are trends that make sense. Study the cues that you get when your intuition gives you information that you can later verify, and notice what is different about the times when your information cannot be verified.

How can you apply intuition to making choices? Let's say you are about to purchase a house. The location is great, the price is right, and the inspection goes well. Friends are telling you that you would be a fool not to take this deal. Yet, there is something about this deal that does not feel right to you although you can't quite put your finger on it. In this case, do you buy the house or do you pass on this opportunity? It is a personal decision because for some people a gut feeling is enough to make a decision, and for others it is not. You can use your intuitive impression as a cue to get additional information about the house. Additional information may reveal the cause of your unease or may provide evidence that you need in order to make a good decision.

If you are not sure what your intuition sounds like, simply record the feelings, desires, images, and memories that come up for you as you consider each of the choices one by one.

Exercise 6: Listening to My Intuition

Let's start with your goal:

_____
_____
_____
_____
_____
_____

What comes to mind for you when you think of this goal? If you see yourself one year from now, do you see whether or not you have accomplished your goal? If yes, what helped you most in achieving it? If no, what were your road blocks? Please don't expect to have factual information here, just write down what comes to mind.

_____
_____
_____
_____
_____
_____

Now consider one of the options that you can choose in order to accomplish your goal:

_____

_____

_____

_____

_____

What thoughts, memories, images, or sensations do you get as you see yourself choosing this option?

_____

_____

_____

_____

_____

Consider a different option that you can choose in order to accomplish your goal:

_____

_____

_____

_____

_____

What thoughts, memories, images, or sensations do you get as you see yourself going down that path?

_____

_____

_____

_____

_____

Repeat this process for all the options as you are making the choice.

 C3

Just as we vary in our ability to distinguish scents and tastes, we vary in our ability to intuit, or perceive signals from the environment. Whether our natural predisposition to intuition is high or low, the more we use intuition, the more adept we become in getting information through it.

STEP 5. GET TO KNOW YOUR INNER COMMUNITY

If someone asks you: "Who are you?" what would you answer? There are many ways to answer this question. One way is to define yourself in terms of your personal interests and preferences: *I am a dancer. I am a healer. I am a writer. I am an avid reader. I am a jazz player.* Another way is to think of yourself in terms of your role in your family or community: *I am a daughter. I am a parent. I am a spouse. I am a friend. I am an aunt. I am a daughter-in-law.* You can define yourself as a professional: *I am an educator. I am a mentor. I am an expert in my field.* You can also define yourself in terms of personal characteristics: *I am an introvert. I am a perfectionist. I am a peacemaker. I am a learner. I am a listener. I am a go-getter.*

I would like for you to search for your answers to this question because it will lead you to making better decisions. Think in terms of nouns rather than adjectives in order to keep your definitions more objective. For example, saying that you are *motherly* is different from saying that you are *a mother.*

Exercise 7: Who Am I? Getting to Know My Inner Community.

Please answer the question "Who am I?" as completely as you can:

I am a _____

I am a _____

I am a _____

I am a _____

I am a _____

I am a _____

I am a _____

I am a _____

I am a _____

I am a _____

Feel free to add more lines. Review your list and meet your *inner community*: the many identities/parts of you that summed up together make you who you are.

CR

Inspired by the explanation of the inner community in Laura Day's book *Welcome to Your Crisis*, I grew to believe that each of our identities has a distinct voice. I am not referring to the dissociative identity disorder in which a person may display multiple personalities that have distinct and separate memories and thoughts. I am talking about the different roles that you play in life, and the ways in which those roles force you to make decisions. For instance, in your role of an Introvert, you prefer to stay home rather than go to a concert, while in your role of a Friend, you are inclined to go to a concert to hear your friend play and support his performance. When you make the decision whether to stay or to go, which *you* will make the call: *you-the-introvert* or *you-the-friend*?

Sometimes, the voices of your identities may sound in unison, but they can also create an unpleasant dissonance. To get through it during the decision-making time, pay close attention to *the person in your inner community* who will be affected most by your choice. If you are taking a high-power job, for example, you-the-professional may prosper while you-the-parent may suffer. When facing a choice, think about the following questions regarding your inner community:

Which member of my inner community...
- *... will be most affected by my choice?*
- *... is in the best position to make the best choice?*
- *... has a hidden agenda related to this choice?*

Impact of Stress and Environmental Factors on Your Decisions

Lawrence Williams, an Assistant Professor from the University of Colorado, and John Bargh, a Yale Psychology Professor, explored the impact of environmental factors on decision-making in their article published in the journal *Science* in 2008. Specifically, they looked at the link between a physical sensation of cold or warmth on emotional perception of warmth. Half of the unsuspecting study subjects were casually asked to hold a cup of hot coffee for several seconds, and the other half were asked to hold a cup of iced coffee for the same amount of time. As a main task, the subjects were asked to evaluate personal characteristics of a target person on a photo. It turned out that the subjects who held the hot cups evaluated the target person as significantly warmer than the subjects who held the cold cups. The subjects' physical sensation of warmth from holding the cups subconsciously translated into an emotional reaction of warmth. Whether you are aware of it or not, factors in your environment can have a great impact on your decisions.

Your state of mind also has a lot to do with the choices that you make. Let's look at a recent study by Stanford Professor Baba Shiv, an influential neuroscientist and a marketing guru. Dr. Shiv demonstrated that "...participants who had been asked to memorize a seven-digit number were much more likely to choose chocolate cake over fruit salad than those who had been asked to memorize only a one-digit number." (Stanford Business Magazine, February 2008.) The participants' choices were explained by the difference in the levels of stress that their brains experienced because of memorizing. So, stress seems to make people more vulnerable to choosing options that are not optimal for them. Our working memory can hold about 7 pieces of information at a time. If you consider the number of things that you keep in mind at any given time, you can imagine the amount of stress that you are constantly under.

Here are a few things that you can do to counteract the impact of the environment and stress on your decisions:

- Be kind to yourself when you make choices; you can only hold yourself responsible for your conscious, not the subconscious. Your choices are not always direct results of your conscious processing.

- Before making a choice, survey your environment: is there anything in your immediate environment that might be affecting your decision? Even though you may not always understand impact of the environment on your choices, plain awareness may help you reason out why you are inclined to choose one thing over another.
- If possible, separate your decision from your current environment as well as from your current state of mind. You can do so by physically moving to a different space and noticing whether your preferences change as your immediate environment changes. You can also put yourself into a different state of mind: close your eyes and imagine that you are on a perfect stress-free vacation; ask yourself what choice you would make from that vacation spot.

In Conclusion

Your goal is crystallized, your options are clearly defined and information is gathered.

Given all of this information, how do you now make a decision? How do you know whether to take your mind's perspective over intuition, or vice-versa? It comes down to this: *you make the decision by choosing to give more weight to points that have the most value and meaning for you.*

There is a lot more that can be said on the topic of choice. For example, when is it the best strategy to wait things out rather than make a decision as soon as possible? Or, how do you forgive yourself for the choices that you made in the past? What is the best way to cope with choices that other people make? How do you make choices as a couple or as a group? What strategy works best for making decisions on the spot? Let's continue this conversation. You can contact me and leave your questions and comments on my website at http://www.AlinaBas.com .

The pay-off for following the five-step systematic approach to decision-making is that you will always know, regardless of the outcome, that you made the best possible decision at the given time. If at a later date your inner judge tells you that you *should have* known better, just remind him or her that *should* is in the dream world. You made the best decision possible in the real world.

cx

I would like to extend my heartfelt gratitude to David, truly the Beloved, and my Mom for having faith in me and being my Home. I am grateful to Misha Leder, Marina Romashko and Lisa Lapush for kindness and support. A special thanks to Vivian Sun for always setting the bar high and inspiring me to reach it. Not least, I want to thank Martha Beck for introducing me to coaching, and being an amazing example of "Live it to give it!"

Alina Bas is a Certified Life Coach who gets called when people need a no-nonsense coach who cares. Alina helps clients breathe life into uninspiring work situations, face tough choices, and find their true calling. In corporations, she coaches GenXers through developing leadership styles that fit their personalities. Alina holds a Master's degree in Industrial/Organizational Psychology from NYU, and has Reiki I and II certifications. She has 10 years of corporate experience in Organizational Development and Training, and currently serves as an internal consultant for the largest municipal healthcare system in the USA. Alina's coaching practice is based in New York City. Her website is http://www.AlinaBas.com.

Please see bibliography on p. 257.

Please see bibliography on p. 257.

CS

A Woman's Energy Crisis and the Essential Art of Self-Love

by Valerie LaPenta Steiger

This is primarily about women, but if you are a man, don't stop reading! You can use these tools to help the women you love. This information can help explain some of the darkness that women encounter when their energy dwindles.

Diane came to me for life coaching because she wanted to change careers and wasn't clear on what she wanted. In typical mid-life fashion, this very smart, very capable fifty-something woman was seeking to find her true purpose. *"Why, did you lose it somewhere?"* my good-intentioned, sarcastic twin wanted to scream. *"Can't you see how smart and capable you ARE? How can you NOT know your purpose?"* I envisioned my Italian hands swinging wildly; one with a slap to the head, the other gesturing, fingers cupped and pointed upward in the "aaayyh, get over it" position. (For a visual depiction, tune in to any Sopranos™ episode!)

It always starts like this. A client comes to me with a stated goal. She needs clarity. Guidance. A gentle smack upside the head! And then, the magic of life coaching begins to unfold. It's almost never about what she initially thought was the problem. Diane (whose name is changed to protect her identity) had a textbook résumé, vast experience, and she really WAS quite clear about her talents. What unfolded beneath her career coaching request, was a full-blown energy crisis! She was stuck – stopped dead in her tracks with her inner battery drained. She possessed everything she needed to reach her goals, except that her "on" switch was stuck on "off." Diane's energy crisis was not much different from the kind you read about in newspapers.

The media is filled with notions of an energy crisis, with critical issues surrounding global warming, depleted resources, and increased energy consumption. Global discussions ensue around developing clean, renewable energy to save our planet, and there is a social trend to engage in a green lifestyle. So, I jump in to comply with this trend. I screw in compact fluorescent bulbs and recycle papers and plastics, and I try really hard to contribute to the cause and not be overwhelmed with guilt should a plastic bottle slip by me. This led me to thinking about similarities with human energy crises and how one source of imbalance in our life can affect many areas, including our efforts to restore balance.

Considering this, I assessed Diane's energy independence (or lack thereof), her energy consumption (or rather what consumed her), and her renewable energy resources (a pint of ice cream and Lifetime Movie Network?) I wondered why so many female clients are overwhelmed, depressed, or exhausted. What sources are they depending on from others? What consumes their energy and makes them require so much self-nurturing reinforcement? And why does it take so much literature and such extreme efforts to renew and recharge? If I could get all my wonderful female clients to shift their energy – to independently generate and renew their energy – in essence lead their own life – could it have a positive impact? Could we, together, come up with a plan for women to change the world?

But wait, before you start conjuring up images of Gloria Steinem and burning bras, let me share a theory that I have about gender differences. My hunch comes mostly from listening to clients, observing experiences, and applying intuition. Of course, scientific research has provided great evidence of physical, psychological, societal, and cultural gender differences. In order to tackle this complex subject, I will need to apply generalizations that wouldn't pass the litmus test of controlled variables in science and research. So, forgive me in advance if I ruffle any gender feathers or step on any scientist toes!

The gap is closing between scientists and new-age philosophy on the discussion of human energy systems or *spirit*, thanks to incredible advances in brain research. I'm fascinated by human energy systems. Perhaps it's no coincidence that I worked for many years in the electric utility industry before I had my own energy crisis, which changed my life direction. I'm interested in the nonphysical energy that animates our cells, creates thoughts and feelings, and connects all living things. Carolyn Myss, author of *Anatomy of the Spirit,* explains the phenomenon,

> "In the human energy system, our individual interactions with our environment can be thought of symbolically as electromagnetic forces. These circuits run through our bodies and connect us to external objects and other people... we are constantly in communication with everything around us through this system."

While human energy systems are certainly universal, they seem to run on different levels or frequencies for women and men. I've observed this trend with female clients, which heightened my curiosity about this difference. Diane provides a good example of this and also the important role of self-love when managing a human energy crisis.

Energy Transmission – Two Frequency Lines

Our electric utility system depends on a complex infrastructure – a network of grids that transmit high voltage from a generation source. There are system operators who are critically important in overseeing the timing and direction of this energy because it can't be stored; rather it is generated as needed and transmitted based on demand.

Our human energy system has a similar rhythm and direction, depending on whether the system operator is male or female. Historically, and still in most parts of the world, men are socially dominant – perceived as stronger, smarter, in control, more valuable. Women, however, have been (and in some places still are) viewed as weaker, less intelligent, submissive, and less valued.

Men appear to lead with an outward energy force, demonstrating strength and acting against fear. I will call this male energy the *P Force*, which summarizes the male social modus operandi (MO) as: Perform, Produce, Provide, Protect.

Women, in contrast, tend to lead with an inward energy force, demonstrating care and acting towards love. Female energy seems to be hard-wired to Create, Cultivate, Communicate, Cooperate – an MO I have labeled the *C Force*.

These two energy forces run parallel to each other, and both are necessary and vital to our existence. Adverse consequences are experienced by both men and women when these energy forces are at peak demand or are extremely out of balance.

Energy Distribution – The Push and Pull of Opposite Forces

In the electric utility world, distribution lines carry energy that has been stepped down from the transmission towers to a lower voltage that is then divided and distributed. Similarly, both male and female energy is divided and distributed, and this can be best explained by Martha Beck's concept of the two selves. One of Martha Beck's predominant themes in *Finding Your Own North Star* is the concept of the Social Self and the Essential Self, and the important role both play in navigating us towards a fulfilling and balanced life. Looking at these two selves as an energy distribution system, we need to be plugged in to both to keep us fully operating and moving in the right life direction. And this is done best when we are *balanced*.

The energy of the Essential Self, as implied, is the very essence of who we are. It is self-generated from DNA – before birth – and it animates us in the form of personality, characteristic desires, preferences, emotional reactions, and involuntary physiological responses. This is our energy's unique frequency level that cannot be changed. As Martha writes, "It would be the same whether you'd been raised in France or China, by beggars or millionaires: it's the basic YOU stripped of options and special features."

The energy of the Social Self is the basis for the skills that we learn. The Social Self is generated outside of us – after birth – and is derived from our surroundings: social approval, cultural norms, societal roles, parental expectations. And because we are highly evolved, social beings, we depend mostly on this energy because it is readily available and gratifying. Its fuel is to please others, be successful, do a really good job, do the "right" thing, etc. Social Self Energy is a terrific asset, since it energizes us to sustain relationships and meet a myriad of financial, career, and personal goals.

But if, in spite of all our achievements, we feel exhausted, discontented, and unfulfilled, this is a clue that our Social Self Energy is overloaded, and we are disconnected from our Essential Self Energy. When these two energy sources are out of balance, there will be a shift in how we think, feel, and act.

Martha Beck refers to the Social Self out of balance as our Dictator, and the Essential Self out of balance as our inner Wild Child. When the Social Self Energy signal is too strong, it will communicate like a dictator: screaming at us to work harder, do better, get more. If the Essential Self energy is the stronger connection – in control without social structure and guidance – it will sound like an uncontrollable child, whining and crying for love and attention.

Transformers – Balancing the Flow

Like transformers – devices that alternate electric circuits when there is a difference in voltage or current – we require a mental device to alternate and balance our energy depending on gender (*P Force* and *C Force*) and energy levels (Essential and Social). In order to explore this, I've illustrated their respective differences using the metaphor of a see-saw. (See illustration on the following page.)

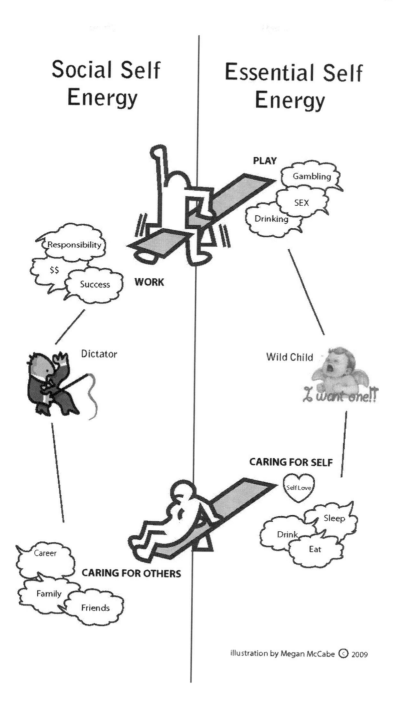

Social Self Energy

Essential Self Energy

PLAY

Gambling

SEX

Drinking

Responsibility

$$

Success

WORK

Dictator

Wild Child

I want one!!

CARING FOR SELF

Self Love

Sleep

Drink

Eat

Career

CARING FOR OTHERS

Family

Friends

illustration by Megan McCabe © 2009

Imagine a see-saw, where the male *P Force* begins in the balanced center. As his energy level increases under the social pressure of Performing, Producing, Providing, and Protecting, the seesaw tips towards what I will summarize as WORK. When the *P Force* is pushed to its capacity, the inner voice of Dictator is in command. For a man this might sound like, "I'm not making enough money," "I'm not climbing the ladder fast enough," or "My hard work isn't noticed." Out of balance, the *P Force* pushes with all its might towards its opposite: PLAY. A man's inner Wild Child will often manifest itself *outwardly* in the form of seemingly playful, but often dangerous risk-taking activities. We've all witnessed the politician on his platform to stomp out immoral behavior, while privately hiring young escorts. Or another who spent an entire political career marked by his anti-gay stance and was then found soliciting gay sex in a public bathroom. Not to pick on politicians, but they are just glorious public examples of the private Wild Child in *all* of us.

On the other side of our social playground is a see-saw where the female *C Force* begins in the balanced center. As her energy level increases under the social pressure of Creating, Cultivating, Communicating, and Cooperating, the seesaw tips towards what I will summarize as CARING FOR OTHERS. Here, at full force, she is exhausted not only from CARING, but also from the invisibility of her efforts that are typically (socially) taken for granted. The inner voice of Dictator gets very personal: "You're such a loser," "You're just not good enough," "You should be ashamed of yourself." In contrast to the *P Force* that pushes with all its might externally towards PLAY, the *C Force* withdraws internally, turning away from its opposite, CARING FOR SELF. The see-saw gets stuck, and the Wild Child shows up trying to comfort, but often with dangerously self-sabotaging behavior. Think of the young celebrity singer who, under pressure, shaved her head and partied uncontrollably, later losing custody of her children. Or another singing artist who was brutally beaten by her boyfriend, and then publicly announced that she had reconciled with him. These are extreme public displays of the Wild Child self-saboteur in *all* of us.

One reason for the contrast in results – and I am generalizing to make a point – is because of the contrasting directions in which these two forces travel. Male energy is typically *working hard* on a physical platform set within linear time. Female energy is *caring hard* and generally running 24/7 in the nonphysical world of nurture and love.

To review, men WORKING and women CARING FOR OTHERS illustrate a broad view of any societal or cultural pressure designed to please others. Likewise, men PLAYING and women *not* CARING FOR SELF (self-sabotage) shows a broad perspective of any acting out behavior. **When either side is pushed to any extreme, it signifies an imbalance or a disconnection.**

Energy Crisis – Revealed

In Diane's case, I suspected that an energy crisis was keeping her from moving forward. It was all too familiar to my life prior to changing careers and becoming a counselor and life coach. I spent a good part of my life out of balance, and I've survived what many female clients go through before they get stuck or break down: abuse, homelessness, living with alcoholism, divorce, single-parenting, financial hardship, death of both parents. My life changed completely when I finally learned and applied what I now call *C Force Wisdom*. I passionately believe this wisdom is inherent in every woman who needs only to reconnect and experience it.

In terms of energy independence, it turned out that Diane was entangled in an abusive, codependent marriage that was draining her *C Force* energy and blocking her ability to self-nurture. She was consumed with worrying about her husband and ruminating, "We were meant to be together... he's just going through a hard time," when in reality, he was openly having affairs for over five years and not coming home for weeks at a time. *Gentle smack upside the head!*

Simultaneously, she cared for an elderly mother with health issues and an adult son who dropped out of college and moved back home, both of which put a strain on finances. Talk about energy consumption! She rationalized her family's difficulties by saying that they all just needed her help. She loved them all, of course, and felt obligated to care for them. In the midst of all of this loving and caring, Diane's *C Force* reached capacity and her inner world began experiencing rolling blackouts – dark episodes of uncertainty, confusion, guilt, and doubt. Inner strength lost, and seesaw stuck, she turned to self-sabotaging behavior that included lots of ice cream and Lifetime Network movies.

Renewable Energy – Light at the End of the Playground

Life, of course, is a continually moving see-saw. A leading mind-body expert, Joan Borysenko said, "The only time we achieve a perfect state of balance is when we're dead." The light inside all of us will never go completely dim. If you recall, Essential Self Energy cannot be changed.

Without words, it will always find a way to communicate. It sends messages in our physical bodies, as in recurring sickness or bouts of chronic pain. Or we may experience a series of strange coincidences; what may appear as accidents or unexpected obstacles – all in the *spirit* of gaining our attention and offering insight that we are disconnected and out of balance.

Energy-drained, Diane was unaware that her Essential Self was still steering her towards her right life! It showed up as a career crisis in a life coach's office. I was not surprised in the least that she recently began having difficulties with a new boss, which put her on this path. Her Essential Self Energy was communicating – just short of smacking her upside the head, screaming *"aaayyh, enough already!"* that she needed to change direction. However, jumping directly into instruction would sound more like a Dictator assigning another "have to" to her already long lists of "shoulds." First, she needed to tap into her own energy sources that were infinitely available and renewable. She needed guidance in self-nurturing and self-care.

A very necessary prerequisite to taking action of any kind is to reconnect to Essential Self Energy and acquire the essential art of self-love. Love is not a skill or technique that comes with instruction. **Love is a direction, an organic ability within us, and without a doubt the most positive, feel-good vibration that our energy system can generate and release.**

Another Martha Beck coach, Jeannette Maw, is a master of the Law of Attraction and advocates the importance of self-love. In her recent e-Book, *The Art of Self-Love: The Essential Key to Successful Manifesting,* she writes, "Self-love is simply the love of one's self." I would add that it is the act of loving both of our selves (Essential and Social) and accepting the totality of who we uniquely are. Jeannette goes on to say, "Self-love is appreciating who you are, feeling good about yourself, directing loving thoughts inward, and being good to yourself through actions."

The problem is not that women don't know how – we certainly demonstrate our ability to love and care for others à la the *C Force*. The problem I have found with many clients is a lack of commitment to our selves. This is because it is so antithetical to *C Force* energy to act selfishly. Yet it's exactly what we need to do to survive and thrive in our natural, feminine light.

Change is a universal challenge that all humans experience, and it's difficult to change an energy force that's been programmed for years. In essence, it requires a change in *identity*. This is terrifying for all of us. We are usually waiting for something to change outside of us (a husband's behavior, a job, etc.) so that we could just get our life back to the way it always was. We may feel our future is uncertain, or are afraid of being judged and losing friends and family. When our energy isn't spent caring for others, it is spent wrestling with our thoughts and feelings, and holding on desperately from falling off the see-saw.

And, all change is cyclical. (Think of the stages of metamorphosis from caterpillar to butterfly.) So, if you feel out of balance and your seesaw is stuck, you can cycle through the following stages to recycle and renew your own *C Force Wisdom*! It involves redirecting each *C Force* component that you already possess. The following plan is a summary of my 3-month coaching program.

A New Energy Plan

C Force Component #1 – Create

Diane's voice escalated with anxiety as she complained about friends telling her to leave her husband; while her priest was telling her she should stay. She sat at the edge of her seat, pushing me to tell her what to do. So, giving her a gentle dose of the authority her Social Self was seeking, I gave her permission to do *nothing*. This stopped Diane dead in her tracks. She was shocked, and later told me, so relieved.

The death of a negative thought, an identity that no longer fits, or a life that is filled with misery isn't something we do; it's something that happens to us. Our mind will race like a Google™ search engine looking for solutions and calling us to action. This is the most difficult challenge we face, because it's counterintuitive to our logical, dominant, Social Self that will be criticizing us, pushing us to do something. But the ONLY thing we need to do – and must do – is relax into it and do nothing.

Create Space. Sit and do nothing for at least 10 minutes each day! Surrender and rest in a way that works for you. Some people enjoy stillness. Others enjoy gentle movement as in walking. Others like a combination of both: sitting still while watching movement, such as a waterfall. Whatever you choose, make sure it is something that requires no effort. As your mind begins to race with thoughts, don't push them away! Practice watching your thoughts, like a TV news crawl, or like cars going by. Say out loud, "I'm having the thought..." Put yourself in the position of observing your thoughts. *From the energy of Observer, notice that you are not your thoughts.*

Create Compassionate Balance. Now, connect to the energy of your two selves that are out of balance. Going back to my see-saw analogy, your rational mind will tell you that the object of the game is to hold one side down so the other goes up. One side must win. One side must be right. *This is a basic human mistake that we inherently make over and over because we forget that we need both selves in order to fully function.*

So, let's go against logic and play a different see-saw game. Imagine on one side a version of YOU dressed as a Dictator. What negative thoughts does she scream at you? Where did she learn these thoughts? Can you remember a time when you first heard the messages she is screaming? How old were you?

Now, on the other side, picture a version of YOU that reacts like a Wild Child. How does she feel when Dictator YOU is screaming? How does she react? Does she rebel and throw a tantrum, or does she run away and hide?

They are both a part of you, and they both have good intentions, right? Dictator YOU wants you to do your best and pushes you to do more. Wild Child YOU just wants to be happy and loved and pushes back to get what she wants. Now imagine them both lifting slightly at the same time, shifting their weight until they are balanced in mid-air, legs dangling, looking straight at each other. Imagine them both smiling and laughing and so proud! Once again, Observer YOU watches from across the playground. Offer them both a loving compassionate wish: *"May you both be happy, may you both be well, may you both be free from suffering."*

Create Affirmation. Practice sitting for at least 10 minutes, leaving behind any thoughts of the past or worries about the future. Bring your five senses into the present moment. Notice what you see, hear, smell, taste, feel in this moment. Repeat one or more of the following:

- I have the ability to generate all the energy I need, when I need it.
- I am the system operator; I choose when and where my energy runs.
- Right now, even if it is a moment of darkness, I am safe.
- If I never changed one thing, the energy of the world would still continue on.

Create Real Feelings. Allow uncomfortable feelings to come up. We are socialized to push away or hide negative feelings, which only exacerbate and make them bigger. Even the loss of a false idea that you believed for so long, will still require a grieving process of denial, anger, sadness, and acceptance. These feelings will dissipate rather quickly if you can notice and describe these feelings out loud with present moment, five-sensory perception. Once the feeling dissolves, you can go back to Observer YOU and find the thought that created the feeling.

C Force Component #2 – Cultivate

Cultivate New Thoughts. When you identify a negative thought that has caused you to feel badly or act harmfully to yourself or others, there is about a 100% chance that the thought was generated from overloaded Social Self Energy. Our brain's wiring system is as complex as our national electric grid, so you can't simply cut the power to these thoughts. You need to gently step down the voltage and transform the energy. This can be accomplished using a process of inquiry, questioning your thoughts that may be limiting or false.

Ask yourself: Is the thought really true? Can you remember the first time you ever had the thought? How does the thought serve you now? How does the thought make you feel or act? Without the thought, would you feel or act differently? Can you find factual, empirical evidence that proves that the thought is not absolutely always true? Applying this evidence, can you restructure the thought to something that is as true or truer? *The instant you state the new thought, your energy will shift, begin to make a new connection, and grow stronger as the old thought fades.*

Cultivate New Energy. As you turn down your Social Self Energy, your Essential Self Energy will organically increase in strength. Without forcing, you may begin to make subtle changes to your outside world; you may redecorate a room, try on a new clothing style, or begin a new hobby or activity. *Imagine. Discover. Play. This is what the Essential Self does best, and without any force or effort from your Social Self, clues will form about what your new life will look like.*

Cultivate A Vision. Create a vision board by posting anything and everything that catches your attention. *Remember, the Essential Self doesn't speak with words; rather it will subtly shift your attention to natural selections of what it wants most. All you need to do is feel it, believe it, and follow it.*

Cultivate Focused Attention. Now that you have set new intentions with new energy generating new thoughts, you can begin to narrow and focus your attention. In order to more fully connect, you will still need to turn down visual cognition (the way we perceive, organize, recognize, search, and remember what we experience visually); and literality – the way we relate, describe, or in other words make meaning of our thoughts using language. This is another exercise to reconnect with your Observer Self. **Observing is critical in untangling the pictures and language we assign to the pain in our life.** The following exercise, practiced daily, will demonstrate a stable, unchangeable, immutable fact – no matter what difficulties come up in life, your non-physical self – call it *energy* or *spirit* or *essence* – is always there, even when you may forget or feel disconnected.

Focus on one object and try to minimize blinking. While staring, notice the air/space between you and the object – actually *look* at the air/space. Using peripheral vision, notice the space to the right of you and the object. Notice the space to the left of you and the object. Notice the space above and below you. Try, with your mind's eye, to imagine the space behind you. At this point, you should feel very fuzzy – keep staring at the object and begin saying its name over and over, i.e. rock, rock, rock, rock until the word as you know it disappears and all you hear is the sound of *rock*. As your vision becomes so fuzzy that you can hardly see, close your eyes and *fall into the space*. Just float into it. When you are ready (usually when thoughts start generating again) take a deep breath, open your eyes, and begin writing – without thinking or forcing – just scribble whatever thoughts, ideas, and images come up. *Right here, you are connected. These thoughts, ideas, images are Essential Self YOU. Listen to this part of you. Trusting what comes up, and committing to it, is the act of self-love.*

C Force Component #3 – Communicate

Armored with new thoughts, recharged energy, a new vision, and focused attention, you are ready for action! This is both very exciting and extremely frustrating!

Communicate Commitment. By now all of your juicy Essential Self Energy has given you enough clues to form a clear picture and direction for your new life. It may be a very simple change, or it may be complex and require a formalized, staged plan. With balanced energy, your Social Self Energy will guide you through action. The important thing is that you communicate a commitment around your intentions. *This is your personal Mission Statement.*

Communicate Confident Action. Be willing to learn something new. This was easier when you were young and naturally growing. Now you're learning new things and unlearning old programming at the same time. This requires patience and courage because you will fail. And you will start over. And you will fail again. It will be OK, because you'll have a confident Mission Statement, and the courage to meet energy shortages (i.e. failures, fears) by recycling back to your **Create** and **Cultivate** components (do nothing, balance with compassion, affirm) that are now plugged in and ready to go! You are ready to take concrete action steps. *This is your new Life Plan.*

C Force Component #4 – Cooperate

With all components plugged in, your new identity will be fully formed and you will be running at 100% capacity. All that is required at this stage is a continuum of balancing, directing, and sustaining your energy system. Running at 100% is both great and challenging at the same time. If you've come this far in the plan, you are very busy and wildly successful. *NOW is the time for self-nurturing and self-care, and you are prepared and ready because you have mastered the essential art of self-love!*

Cooperate with Body. Practice relaxation techniques, pamper yourself with spa treatments, engage in physical activities you enjoy, and take pleasure in your sexuality.

Cooperate with Mind. Manage stress. Continue to practice mindfulness exercises and meditations to challenge limiting beliefs and return to Observer.

Cooperate with Spirit. Keep a gratitude journal. Be grateful every day for the smallest and biggest of things. More importantly, connect your energy with the energy of others. Change your stance from CARING FOR OTHERS to SERVING OTHERS. *Lead your energy with abundance and love, and offer it back so that others can recharge and renew.*

The Energy Cycle

Whether we're in an energy crisis or at the height of mastering self-love, it's all about communication – how we connect with our nonphysical self. After working with me for several months, Diane stood up to her abusive husband and filed for divorce. She left her corporate job for a much more fulfilling position at a non-profit agency. The last time I spoke with her, she reported that her days were filled with *passion* and she felt a sense of *freedom*.

If we equate ENERGY to SPIRIT, then I can summarize this plan in this way: The first two parts (Create and Cultivate) are **how SPIRIT talks to us**. The last two (Communicate and Cooperate) are **how we talk to SPIRIT**. This is a very important conversation. Energy crises will occur. Life is a continually moving see-saw. We won't be able to operate at 100% forever. There will be events that will, once again, overload or cut off our energy – throwing us out of balance or into darkness. With a solid commitment, the perfected art of self-love, and a conscious connection to our infinite energy source, I believe that women could indeed change the world – for the better – *and without burning a single bra!*

✣

Gratitude and love go to my amazing daughter and Illustrator, Megan, and my talented stepdaughter and "Ghost" Editor, Samantha. And of course to Glenn, who shares my life and tolerates my insomnia writing attacks. And to my spaghetti-eating dogs, Sophia (Loren) and Gina (Lollobrigida), who remind me every day to go out and play.

Valerie LaPenta Steiger, MA, LAC, CLC, is owner of VLS Consulting, Inc. and MegaJoy Professional Life Coaching. She's a licensed counselor (AZ); certified life coach (Martha Beck, PhD); author, and speaker. Her expertise on women in transition -- specializing in overcoming obstacles, accepting change, and achieving goals – comes from personal experience. She's gone through and survived most of the issues her clients are dealing with and finds deep purpose and joy in letting others know there is a way out. Valerie provides coaching, seminars and workshops, and publishes a free e-zine, *Shift Happens! Navigating Through Life's Changes.* She maintains offices in Mesa, AZ and Santa Clarita, CA. Visit www.mega-joy.com.

Editing provided by Samantha Smith. Visit www.smith-ofwords.com.

Please see bibliography on p. 257.

CB

Our Brain When We Grieve

Why Loss Hurts So Much… and What We Can Do About It

By Polly O'Connor

You're driving home – thinking of nothing in particular, your mind blessedly numb. All of a sudden, the ever-present pervasive molten core of sadness-horror-fear-loss swells into a tidal wave of pain… the intensity squeezes your lungs so you can barely breathe. Your brain is flooded with images and thoughts of your Loved One. You are filled with longing to see and feel and hear them again. Your body aches with sadness. The reality that they are gone, and you'll never see them again tortures your brain. Tears sting your eyes and your clenched throat chokes back a sob as the images and feelings become almost overwhelming.

ಛ

It was the tidal waves of pain after my beloved John died that compelled me to search out why loss hurts so much. And, what I could do about it. This is what I learned.

Loss is experienced by the brain and felt in the body. Our grief is very individual and will be made harder or easier by our genes, upbringing, previous loss, current circumstances, finances, and more.

A few of the losses we might grieve are:

- Obvious: special person (spouse, partner, child, parent, close friend), pet, job, home;
- Not so obvious: dream, health, change in comfortable/familiar daily routine;
- Ambiguous/caught between celebrating and grieving: alive but permanently injured, a loved one is missing but there's cause for hope, the 'empty-nest' syndrome.

(For simplicity, I'll use the term "Loved One" to cover all loss.)

The simple techniques I discovered can minimize our pain and sadness; they can allow us to heal while still honoring and holding onto our memories. Just understanding the process can help.

If we have lost our job or home, seeing an office building or a design magazine can trigger a physical and emotional reaction. If our pet has died, catching sight of the bare spot on the kitchen floor where the water bowl used to be can do it. Why does that happen? Have we gone insane? Are we weak? Are we overreacting and being too emotional?

ℭℨ

Why Loss Hurts So Much

Neural Connections – Our Loved One is Ingrained in Our Very Being

Scientists learned decades ago how our brain cells (called neurons) create connections in our brain. When we have an experience – when we see something, hear something, feel something, smell something, sense something – the connected neurons in 'neural pathways' make sense of it, decide what to do, and then implement or inhibit a behavior.

In a brilliant manifestation of the brain's talent for efficiency, the connections not only increase, they strengthen the more the experience is repeated. Soon, the processing of each and every aspect of it becomes faster, easier, smoother. Ultimately, with enough repetition, it becomes automatic, and we are barely aware of the process.

Remember when you moved into your current home? You deliberately decided on the best spot in the bathroom to put the tube of toothpaste you would use each day. At first, you had to consciously reach for that medicine cabinet door; maybe you tried to open it the wrong way a couple of times. Now, you might sometimes wonder, after you've left the bathroom, "Did I brush my teeth already?"

The process has become so ingrained in your neural pathways that you reach for the tube of toothpaste and even brush your teeth on "autopilot."

It's only if the toothpaste tube is not there, in its usual spot, that you notice it. You stand there blankly for a moment, hand poised in air, as your brain works out what's wrong. At the same moment that your subconscious is alerting you the tube is missing, it is busy retrieving all the possible explanations and offering them up to your consciousness. You may give a little start as you remember, "Aha! It was empty and I threw it out and I need to get the spare tube."

To get a sense of your ingrained pathways, try brushing your teeth with your other hand. See how "wrong" that feels? Now switch back to your usual hand. It feels comfortable, normal, right.

The same neural process happens with experiences involving our Loved One. Being in the same room with them creates connections in our brain. Seeing them creates connections. Interacting with them over and over increases and strengthens the connections until every aspect of our involvement with that person is ingrained as smoothly and wonderfully familiar as a well-worn, well-loved garden path. Every detail of them and of our experiences with them truly becomes part of us.

Neurochemicals – The Spice of Life

Meaning is added to those details via our brain chemicals. Neurochemicals are like the spices that add pizzazz to our food. They can make our experiences bitingly bitter or exquisitely delicious... and every flavor variation in between of feelings / emotions / physical sensations.

We feel warm, safe, deeply joyful, content when we are happily with our Loved One – because the brain has released oxytocin and/or endorphins.

Give it a try right now: visualize someone who gives you great joy. Do you feel the subtle change in your facial muscles, around your eyes, the corners of your mouth, your heart, your stomach?
That's how it feels to be embraced by oxytocin.

The brain has evolved to react this way because being with someone special, bonding with that safe someone, meant Survival. In humankind's early history, living on our own meant certain death. We needed a group to survive. One lone person could not hunt down and kill a woolly mammoth plus gather enough seeds and berries and water; one could not ensure safety; one person alone could certainly not populate the earth.

Our brains make bonding overwhelmingly enticing and rewarding by producing incredibly wonderful neuro-chemicals. It then imprints in our neuron connections the memory of the chemicals' effects so that we will repeat the good, beneficial experiences.

So, it's not only the images of our Loved One that are imprinted in our brain without our conscious awareness or deliberate actions. The feelings and emotions we felt when we saw them are also ingrained, in our very being.

Millions of Memories, Billions of Bits: Stored in Our Brain

Imagine your Loved One at, for example, the kitchen table. Think of as many experiences as possible that involved them there: sitting there next to them – the family around during holidays. How many memories can you retrieve, involving them and that table?

Pick a single moment from one of those memories. Observe how many details are in that 'snapshot' moment – include all the sights / sounds / smells / tastes / touches / emotions / locations / other events that were happening at the same time / the time of year, the time of day / what you were talking about / the twinkle in their eye / how you felt.

Now, how many memories can you come up with if you count each and every experience, interaction, conversation you ever had with them – from the very beginning? Millions?

Those millions of memories that we were aware of when they were happening – with all the billions of details – are filed away in our brain. Since we have approximately 100 billion neurons, each sending signals to about 10,000 other neurons, creating trillions of connections, our brain can certainly handle all those memories, as well as the exponentially more that did *not* make it into our awareness. Our subconscious – constantly scanning the environment – sends upward only a minute amount of information it is processing. If the brain didn't have that usually helpful selective function, we would be overwhelmed with the amount of data our senses receive. However, even if we are not consciously aware of those bits, many get filed away as memories and can be triggered just as easily as the 'aware' ones.

A Cascade of Memories and Pain – Triggered by One Tiny Little Detail

You're in your kitchen and, as you turn to leave the room, your eye catches a glimpse of the kitchen table.

Your brain is immediately bombarded by memory after memory of your Loved One... sitting with them at the table, chatting, eating, laughing – so wonderful – and, trying to change the impossible-to-reach bulb in the light fixture over the table... never an easy exercise but always special because it was something you did together, as a team, you loved helping them and being with them, and it gave you such wonderful warm and happy sensations.

Every cell in your body writhes in pain from the deep and huge longing for your Loved One and for those glorious sensations. The facts assault you – they are gone – forever – never coming back – off the face of the earth – how could that be!! Instead of feeling enfolded by the incredible neurochemicals that created those wonderful warm and happy sensations, you almost double over in pain as the stress chemicals surge through your body. Your muscles tense, your heart and stomach feel like they're in a vise, your throat tightens, scary thoughts career around your brain like acid-coated pinballs in an arcade game of horror: What will you do without them... How can you bear never seeing them again... Never see them again....

Tears, triggered by chemicals like acetylcholine, overflow, and you find yourself once again reaching for the tissues.

That onslaught of images and emotions does not slowly and gently enter our awareness. We don't purposely trigger it – we aren't deliberately thinking, "Here I am, looking at the kitchen table, and my Loved One isn't here, I'm so sad they're gone, poor me. Let me now retrieve many memories that make me sadder."

It is an immediate, physically painful ambush that begins in the deep parts of our brain without any intention on our part.

What could trigger that ambush?

What could possibly be such a dramatic and forceful stimulant?

The short answer: one tiny little detail.

One tiny little detail can cause an entire cascade of memories and physical sensations. How does that happen? WHY does that happen?

How the Ambush Happens

When the brain starts down our well-worn neural pathway of (for example) seeing the kitchen table, it will, in a way, be stopped in its tracks. It cannot make the next, expected ingrained fact/feeling/emotion connection because one tiny little detail is now *different* – 'missing' – changed, because of our loss.

Like the kitchen table is lacking your Loved One's presence...

The brain, in a sense, collides with the reality of the loss – which is distressing.

In addition, the brain must now create NEW connections: we don't stop seeing the kitchen table; we need to create new neural pathways of the table without the image of Loved One there ever again. These new connections are actual, physical changes in our brain that we can experience as anxiety and distress.

The subconscious notices the distress and tries to figure out what's wrong by using techniques that have been so successful to our survival throughout history they continue to this day. Survival – of the individual and therefore the species – is a major, innate motivator of the brain. It's a very powerful instinct in all beings. Unfortunately, when we are grieving, these techniques can ambush us.

We are rarely aware of noticing the stimulus (the kitchen table); we only become aware when the brain's spontaneous attempts to help cause a flood of memories to burst into our awareness:

1. In order to provide information to help us figure out what's different – what's wrong – our subconscious matches up the stimulus with the billions of memory-bits stored away in the depths of our brains. It offers up to us entire memories – with details and feelings – that have even *one tiny* bit that is similar and possibly relevant. This is usually a great survival technique. Unfortunately, what is relevant in our case is the reality of our significant loss – which is DISTRESSING.

2. The brain automatically retrieves memories that match our current mood. This can save precious time in an emergency: retrieving memories that have relevancy to the current situation. But, if we're distressed, DISTRESSED memories will be triggered.

3. Each time a memory is deliberately or spontaneously retrieved and brought into consciousness, new and current information is attached to it. This brain

function can turn our special memories into distressing ones by updating them with all the emotions and facts and import of the reality of our loss and then restoring them in the brain, ready for future retrievals. Before our loss, thinking of a certain vacation spot gave us pleasure; now, that same memory, with the bits of grief and loss attached to it, triggers sadness. We have 'lost' a special memory, and we've added another distressing memory to the storage banks. Our psyche is bombarded with MORE distressed memories.

4. Our brain provides us with as many explanations as possible for our feeling distressed. This is truly efficient when it is on target – but now there are LOTS of distressed memories flooding our mind.

5. The memories we were previously unaware of can be triggered, flooding us with EVEN MORE distressed memories plus profound regret at not having noticed those special aspects of our Loved One; this adds ADDITIONAL distress because we didn't get to enjoy them at the time, we never said "thank you."

One tiny little detail – one 'missing' connection – causes all of that.

A flood of memories can also be triggered by a stimulus-bit matching up with one of the billions of bits stored in our memory banks.

A stimulus-bit – like your hearing the first few notes of a familiar song. At the moment you become aware of hearing the music, your mind is flooded with detailed memories... of the first time you heard it... of something important or significant that was happening when the song was playing... of what clothes you were wearing, where you were, whom you were with, and how you were feeling at the time. Without any deliberate action on your part, you are actually experiencing those emotions again.

Returning to the example at the beginning of this chapter, there were an endless number of missing connections and stimulus-bits during that drive: our reaching the spot where we normally phoned to say we were almost home; passing the little restaurant where we always had our special, celebratory dinners; our internal clock registering the time when we normally would be home and seeing them; reaching for something on the passenger seat and the movement reminding us of reaching for their hand to hold it.

Every infinitesimal detail that even remotely involved our Loved One is deeply rooted – with the accompanying emotions/feelings – in our memory banks and in our neural pathways. Every infinitesimal detail is a potential stimulus creating infinite opportunities for the sudden unexpected unbidden flood of pain and memories.

The more often we phoned home at that certain spot on the drive home and/or the more intense the experience (hearing our Loved One's voice so happy that we are almost home), the deeper and more vivid the imprint, and the more intense the flood.

Our brain is not trying to punish us for having loved or for having grown comfortable in our job or home. It's simply that our very normal reactions to a significant loss trigger the ancient survival mechanisms that proved remarkably efficient over the ages in helping us survive an emergency.

Why the Ambush Happens in a Non-emergency

Beneath our awareness, sensory input from a stimulus, like seeing the kitchen table, first travels to the thalamus, a kind of neural Grand Central Station. From there, most of the sensory signals go on to their relevant parts of the brain for processing. The signals then work their way through the various brain regions and, if it's decided that defensive action is required, an alert to set the body in motion goes to one of the most ancient and fascinating parts of our brain: the amygdala.

However!! At the same moment the signals left Grand Central Station for the above journey, a signal had leapt from the thalamus directly to the amygdala – across one single synapse (the junction between two neurons). To ensure our survival, the primitive amygdala is on constant alert for danger and, ever-vigilant, it errs on the side of caution. It reacts instantaneously – both to external stimuli (the kitchen table) and internal stimuli (our thoughts, emotions) and, because it has not evolved enough from the years of our being vulnerable to saber-tooth tigers, it too often overreacts unnecessarily. If there is anything even remotely dangerous about that stimulus, the amygdala will spring into action.

Why does this matter to us when we have experienced a loss?

The amygdala views loss as danger.

Having a partner, pet, friend, status, good health is considered by the amygdala to be important for survival. The frequently followed, ingrained, well-worn neural pathways of familiar routines or surroundings equate with safety. The interruption or loss of any of those is suspect – and the amygdala will respond, with alarm.

It sends out urgent commands via the release of stress chemicals to enable us to fight-flee-freeze. The chemicals surge through our body causing physical changes. The subconscious, still working on whether or not the threat is valid, interprets the surge of stress chemicals as "something is wrong, we're under attack!" We can't fight or flee from reality or from our thoughts, but it still sends out more stress chemicals to help us fight-flee-freeze – which is sensed by the brain – and we are now in a chronic stress loop and feeling dangerous physical pain.

Have you ever had a police car pull up behind you and turn on their flashing lights? Have you ever realized your wallet is missing – you must have left it at the store! – filled with credit cards and cash? Has another driver ever stupidly or aggressively cut you off? Remember how you felt? Your heart starting racing… your muscles tensed… you could almost hear your blood pounding in your brain.
That's your amygdala reacting – on its own – not to saber-tooth tigers, but to just perceived danger.

Since distressing thoughts are taken as real threats, the brain will urgently attempt to explain/discover the cause of the emergency and save us. The stress chemicals alone can keep us feeling mildly anxious to flat out terrified; add them to the flood of distressing memories, and they can quickly spiral us into scary almost primal thoughts: How could that happen! What will I do without my Loved One! What will happen to me! What's that noise!

The chemicals inhibit the executive part of our brain, the prefrontal cortex, so our memory, decision making, self-discipline, thought processes, and much more are greatly diminished.

We are physically, emotionally, mentally fatigued – a natural byproduct of grief.

We feel sad, so deeply sad that we've lost someone/something very special and important... and foolish for being so afraid, especially if we are normally self-confident... and frenetic with the weird sense of time being limited... and, annoyed and impatient for *still* being pummeled by the pain and sadness... and full of regret for not having done more for and with the Loved One, even if there is absolutely nothing more we could have done.

These, and more, are very common reactions. (The increased incidence of illness and death after a significant loss is well documented.)

No wonder loss hurts so much!

☃

The Good News

The brain does so much subconsciously when we grieve, but we can choose to take gentle actions and use specific techniques that are respectful to our Loved One and will help us heal from the loss. Grief is a natural part of life; some of it is an automatic process that we can soften solely by understanding it. The brain can be deliberately calmed, the stress chemicals intentionally decreased, and the memories tempered so the intensity and frequency of flooding is minimized.

We can form a new life. It will be a different life, but it can be good – even happy.

I promise.

What We Can Do About the Pain of Loss

These are a few of the 'assignments' I give my clients that work no matter what the loss. Some may seem far too simple to be of much help, but they are remarkably effective.

1. Breathe

This is so powerful and couldn't be simpler or more convenient. It's especially helpful if you're having problems sleeping.

As you slowly inhale, feel your lungs expanding as they fill with air. Slowly exhale and feel your lungs deflating. Slowly inhale. Slowly exhale. Gently focus on how your lungs feel as they naturally, rhythmically expand and deflate.
Do as long and as often as you need.

(The science behind this is explained in the invaluable book, *The Mindful Way through Depression*, by Jon Kabat-Zinn et al.)

The reason this helps: when the stress chemicals are making us feel anxious or our brain is flooded with distressing or sad images, choosing to switch our attention to our breath actually sends the brain down a different neural pathway, interrupting the stress loop. The brain cannot continue to think stressful thoughts at the same time we are gently paying attention to our lungs expanding and deflating.

2. Get a Neurochemical "Hit"

Connect with friends (a bonus: this calms the frightened areas of the brain; being with others who are safe is a very important survival mechanism). Volunteer at a humane society or adopt a pet. Get a massage. Go for a run. Bask in the sun. Surround yourself with color. Meditate. Rent a funny video.

(These are from the brilliant and pithy *How to Survive the Loss of a Love* by Peter McWilliams et al.)

The reason this helps: any of these will trigger the release of the oxytocin and endorphins that make us feel comforted and safe. The brain **loves** oxytocin and endorphins, so much so that we actually miss their effect. When our loss takes away an important catalyst for those good neurochemicals, we can suffer a kind of withdrawal and are motivated to replicate them by any means possible: the healthy activities above; or alcohol, sugar, or other "drugs of choice."

3. Consciously Lessen the Pain of the Memories

Anytime a sad memory comes to mind, purposely bring up warm sensations of love and remembrance. It might seem difficult at first, but try to create a feeling state of gratitude for having had this very special person in your life. Think of some specific lessons you've learned and experience you've gained. Purposely come up with as many good thoughts and feelings as you can while keeping that memory in

mind. Imagine 'decorating' the memory with many
wonderful new bits of gratitude and love. When
you are done, visualize re-storing the memory, then
purposely and gently switch your attention to your
breath.

The reason this helps: choosing to purposely and consciously associate more positive, happier meanings to a sad memory will diminish/dilute its painful effects. This sometimes happens naturally with the passage of time. However, we can speed up the process by deliberately changing a memory – whether it was purposely retrieved or it arose spontaneously into our consciousness – from being one of sadness and pain into a more diverse one of perhaps still some residual pain and sadness but also joy and relief and laughter and fondness and gratitude. The next time that memory surfaces, it will have some of the new "encoding." The more this exercise is repeated, the less and less distressing the memory will become.

What an amazing feature of our brain!

4. Discover Our True Goal

Having a significant life change forced upon us is an excellent opportunity to reappraise our journey-to-date and decide to go in a completely new direction or make many little tweaks to our current life.

Devote time to uncovering what YOUR ideal journey
is. Read Martha Beck's books and columns that mix
practical advice with brain science – in a very user-
friendly way – to help you move forward. Dr. Beck is
incredibly brilliant, insightful, compassionate, and
hysterically funny.

Hire a Life Coach.

The reason this helps: having a goal to focus on creates completely new and different neural pathways than the sad, possibly hopeless ones. It proves to us that our journey is not over, it is never too late, and there is always hope for another wonderful life. Remember that farmer's daughter from a small village near Vermont, educated in a one-room schoolhouse, who started painting quaint pictures when she was 76 years old? If Grandma Moses could begin a new career at that age and become one of the most famous artists of all time, then we also can start a new life – at any time!

5.   Purposely Interrupt the Chronic Stress Loop

After John died, I became more and more anxious when driving. After reading *Open Focus* by Les Fehmi and Jim Robbins, I realized that the cataclysmic realities of his death had pushed me into a narrowly focused mode.

Well, it's very difficult driving that way! Besides reducing the field of vision, narrow-focused attention engages the fight-flight-freeze response, and the stress chemical loop begins, bringing along an underlying, hugely anxious state of expecting anything to happen – without a moment's notice – completely and grossly unfair to the entire universe – disastrous – beyond anyone's control. Every oncoming car could potentially swerve into our lane… at every bend a deer could suddenly bound out of the woods directly into our path. It was not inconceivable. After all: if someone so amazingly alive and present and important and special and loved could completely disappear from the face of the earth, then all laws of predictability and fairness had to have been completely shattered.

Until we consciously do something to break the stress loop, it will continue and can worsen. Fehmi's very easy *Open Focus* exercise interrupts that cycle. Read the following, then lay this book down, and give it a try:

Look at any item in front of you. Without shifting your eyes from the item, allow yourself to be aware of the space to the right and to the left of it.
Let your peripheral field of vision widen spontaneously at its own pace to take in that awareness. Once you develop that awareness, enjoy it for a few seconds.
Now, gradually begin to sense the space above and below the item.
In a few moments, still without shifting your eyes, allow yourself to be aware of the three-dimensional space between your eyes and the item.
Finally, become aware of the space all around you.

And, that's it. This exercise can be done almost any place, any time.

The reason this helps: expanding our three-dimensional visual awareness of space creates a change in the way we are paying attention from narrow to open focus, which diminishes the stress chemicals in our brain and body. Our breathing may ease and the muscles in our face, neck, and around our eyes relax. We feel better and our brain works better.

6.   Be Patient and Gentle With Our Self!!

Many of our cultures have grown accustomed to instant gratification and avoiding pain at all costs. But, our life – changed by loss – is full of new neural connections being made, which takes time and can be felt as frustration, anxiety, distress.

Remember when you first used your new cell phone? Was it hugely frustrating and distressing until you learned the location and sequence of its controls, how to search for a programmed number, how to retrieve a message?
After repeating the steps over and over – by necessity if you wanted to use the phone – you now barely have to think to make a call. Healing from loss is the same principle, just incredibly more distressing.

In our new life, maybe we have to take out the trash – always done by our Loved One. It is surprisingly painful to have to do that in the beginning; gradually we "get used to it" as the new neural connections are created and then strengthened through repetition. Soon, the task becomes more familiar and more comfortable.

Until then:

Give yourself permission to grieve. Be patient, be gentle. You deserve it. Be comforted by the knowledge that the sharp edges of the pain WILL soften over time.

Follow the wonderful advice in How to Survive the Loss of a Love by Peter McWilliams et al; it can be downloaded free from www.mcwilliams.com/books/ books or purchased at bookstores/online.

Read about others' experiences, such as Elizabeth Harper Neeld's very wise Seven Choices, Mark Twain's piercing essay about his daughter, The Death of Jean, and other books listed on my website, www. pollyoconnor.com.

Call a friend who will understand.

When necessary, allow yourself a full blown Pity Party. You HAVE suffered a loss. You MISS them! That is the reality!! And it DOES hurt. Allow yourself to give into the longing. Weep if you feel like it: stress-induced tears actually remove toxic substances from the body.

Be amazed at how your eyes deal with excess tears: besides overflowing the bottom lid and pouring down your cheeks, they drain via the tear ducts into your nasal cavities – that's why you need to blow your nose when you cry.

Write a letter to your Loved One – to keep forever in your journal or destroy whenever. Write down all the reasons you are grateful for having had them in your life, and how each reason will help you create and develop your own journey.

Then rest.

The reason these work: by respecting our grief and our Loved One, we validate our natural reactions to loss which comforts, reassures, and allows our brain to relax and dissipate the stress chemicals. We are freed to move forward to more positive, uplifting neural and literal pathways.

The Paradox

With the passage of time, we will begin to notice there are some aspects of Life-Without-Our-Loved-One that are... well, I never know what to call them. Kate Braestrup describes this paradox so perfectly and beautifully in her book, *Here If You Need Me*, about the death of her husband, Drew:

Death alters the reality we inhabit; the death of an intimate changes it completely. No part of my life, from my most ethereal notions of God to the most mundane detail of tooth brushing, was the same after Drew died. Life consisted of one rending novelty after another.

Still, as time went on, some of these novelties proved to be blessings. And I had to learn to live with a paradox.

If Drew had lived, I would not have gone to seminary, would not be ordained, would not have become the Warden Service chaplain. There were places that would have gone unvisited and friends I would never have met.

So while on one hand there is my darling Drew, whom I will never cease to love and never cease to long for, on the other hand there is this wonderful life that I enjoy and I'm grateful for.

I can't make these two realities – what I've lost... what I found – fit together into some tidy pattern of divine causality. I just have to hold them on the one hand... on the other hand: just like that.

Your life will swing suddenly and cruelly in a new direction, and if you are really wise – and it's surprising and wondrous how many people have this wisdom in them – you will know enough to look around for love. It will be there, standing right on the hinge, holding out its arms. And if you are wise, you will fall against it and be held.

From Here If You Need Me by Kate Braestrup. Copyright © 2007 by Kate Braestrup. By permission of Little, Brown & Company.

It is just like that. A paradox.

○ఢ

Conclusion

We will never be the same person after a significant loss. We may, however, discover that we have emerged infinitely stronger – and that we like this new person better.

Our brain when we grieve can keep all the wonderful memories, embrace all the lessons we learned from having known our Loved One, and move us forward to create a most beautiful journey of our own.

As Anaïs Nin wrote in her poem, *Risk*:

And then the day came,
when the risk
to remain tight

in a bud
was more painful
than the risk
it took
to Blossom

ᏣᏃ

I wish you a life filled with Blossoms.

ᏣᏃ

There's not enough room here for me to even attempt to adequately express my gratitude and appreciation to the individuals who helped support me during those times when my brain was grieving. I am blessed to have such amazing angels. You know who you are. I thank you, forever, from the bottom of my heart.

Polly O'Connor had already been helping people solve problems and move forward in life in the decades before earning her formal Life Coach certification from Martha

Beck in 2005. Her compassion and respect for others' journeys, her innate organizing skills and rational thinking, and information she gathered while researching the brain in grief and trauma translate beautifully to helping us in every challenge we might face. Polly spent over thirty years in corporate life, organized home and corporate offices with her consulting business, was associated with an inspirational self-defense program, and earned her business degree from Pace University. For more information, please see her website, www.PollyOConnor.com, and her blog, www.OurBrainWhenWeChange.com.

Please see bibliography on p. 257.

&

Motorcycle Medicine

Healing the Soul on the Road

by Karen Allen

I jump on my motorcycle to connect to the power place within. Only there can I open the space for my innermost desires to come forth – to let my soul speak and be heard. Only there am I safe to confront my fears, be myself, and take my garbage to the curb. Intuitively, we all know this place – this still, quiet place exists within all of us. I use Motorcycling as a vehicle to take me there, to take me back home.

I invite you to come along for the ride! I want to take you into my heart, so you can find the beauty, wonder, and joy of becoming one with your passion and one with every-thing else that exists in your world. I want to help you draw your own road map which will lead you back home to your heart.

"Medicine" is a Native American term for that which heals us and connects us to life. I'm taking motorcycling to a new level and making it a Medicine Ride; riding the back roads with purpose, finding the signs which assist in healing the soul and in bringing forth insight, heightened awareness, and wisdom. I am the Pathfinder who shares the knowledge of the way through the forest so the path may be clear for other travelers; I assist others in finding the courage to explore possibilities and go where less bold spirits dare not tread. This is how I have chosen to put many of my gifts and talents together into one form that will touch the hearts of many.

Following My Own Road Map

I spent the majority of my life letting other people think for me. That's pretty much how a lot of us were raised; parents, teachers, media, society all dictating, directing, approving, disapproving, coercing, and shaming. I grew up to be a master of running away from the true essence of me, drowning out my own voice with the voices of everyone else around me. Follow-the-leader is the name of that game. I don't like it; never did.

I have experienced the greatest motorcycling moments following my own lead. It took years for me to discover that the real desire to ride has been my soul's longing for a connection to life – to get out there and become aware of and appreciate the gifts which constantly surround me – to tap into the energy where I feel my interconnectedness to everything. The desire for that connection is so strong that I'll get out there in unfavorable riding conditions – be it rain, cold, or extreme heat – just to experience it. I think the soul has us searching for whatever it takes to get out of our heads and into our hearts. When we find it, the Universe responds.

Riding a motorcycle is my favorite way of finding that connection. So, I get out there and do it every chance I get. The more I practice making that connection on the open road, the easier it becomes, no matter where I am.

Yearning to Ride

My heart recognized the calling before my head realized it. I had a strong sense from the start, that this is what I wanted to do. I didn't even need to know why – I just knew there was something big in this for me. Riding has also forged the trails to my personal growth. In using the open road as my foremost teacher and guide, I gain a deeper understanding of my existence and that of all which surrounds me. It is in that space I heal my heart by releasing my grief, anguish, and disappointments to the wind. I want to show you where my heart takes me as I travel the winding back roads through forests and farms, over rivers and streams, under hawks and eagles, so you can learn to listen to the messages they have for you and experience the peace they invoke.

Anticipation of the Open Road

I've been in the process of personal transformation since the day I jumped in the saddle. One mile at a time, I've become more of who I truly am by feeding my soul and letting it come alive. Each time I get back in the saddle, I go right back there again – a little longer each time. I have trudged along the same old highway so many times; listening to the voices of others seemingly etched into my head. The more I get out on my motorcycle onto the open road – seeking adventure and new territory – the more I discover myself. This ride I'm on isn't about anyone else. It's about me finding my own way home – riding free.

I get on my bike to practice presence – it's easier for me out there. The more I practice on the road, the easier it is to bring that experience back into the busyness of my daily life. I'm out there learning how to question my mind's chatter and let go of the thoughts and beliefs I've been letting dictate my life. I find that silent space which resides beneath the chatter, and I connect with it. It is within that space that magical things happen. Synchronicities become commonplace. The beauty of me is reflected back by the hundreds of faces I meet. I've traveled the most awesome roads and encountered countless breathless experiences. When I practice living my days the way I ride my motorcycle, magic happens there as well.

The open road is where I practice allowing my heart to be my roadmap. That's the adventure I anticipate: getting out there to feel and be, celebrating newness and freshness rather than intellectualizing and doing. The open road freed me from the outdated mode I had been programmed to operate from.

I use my motorcycle as a *vehicle* to help me reclaim my Self: the part of me that has been with me since birth; the part of me that is beneath the programming and the conditioning. My motorcycle is a tool for personal transformation. It's where I practice letting my heart take the lead. It's where I learn to accept what is. It's the epitome of inspiration – inhaling spirit – for miles on end. When I allow the act of motorcycling to fill me with the pure joy and excitement of being, I become inspired. As motorcycling takes on a whole new perspective, so do I.

I'm not just riding a motorcycle – I'm also connecting to Life out there. The bliss isn't all in the riding. It's also in tapping into the spirit that's been lying dormant and covered.

A Natural Connection

As human beings, we share an innate connection to all of life. We're all searching – our souls longing for us to make a connection to what is larger than ourselves in every given moment, whether we're conscious of it or not. Passion is the soul's calling to make that connection.

Motorcycling is my retreat time. It's the time I reconnect with and replenish myself by making a connection with the Universe. I'm one with it all out there. No physical barriers other than a windshield and glasses. I'm totally free, riding with the wind, once again awakening my spirit which gets easily sidetracked in day-to-day living. I'm just cruising, knowing that the two wheels between me and the pavement are connecting me to all that exists.

Riding Free

I resonate with my motorcycle. Adverse weather conditions are great teachers that have forced me to practice living in the moment. Challenging physical conditions let me know its time to pay attention to the details right here, right now. No time to be lost in worrying about my past and future. They force me to change my focus immediately. The idle chit-chat in my head disappears. I am now one-on-one with the elements. This is real fear and it's all happening right now. This is where I learn about humility, where I taste my vulnerability and see that I really can't control anything outside of myself. This is where I gear up, buck up and take everything I've got inside to move through it. This is the point where I know the only true shelter I have comes from within. This is where I practice surrender. This is where I cry "Uncle" and let the wind and the rain whisk my resistance away until the only option left is to keep going.

When the mind chatter consumes me, I know it's time to hit the pause button and allow nature to be my teacher and sedative. Observing it clears my mind, and encourages my heart to open. In that stillness, I hear that small voice inside of me speak the truth and refuse all doubt. Nature is constantly showing me how to live my life. When I listen to the river and watch it flow gracefully and effortlessly forward, never allowing obstacles to stop it, I am encouraged to persevere regardless of what appears to be in my way.

Rolling along the highway through a grove of aspens, I hit the engine kill switch to listen to the leaves dance with the wind. They aren't fighting it or cursing it. They just flow and bend with it, becoming stronger as they grow.

Embracing Fear

After 11 days on the road, the sweet voices of my children were calling to me. Determination to blast through South Dakota in a day filled me. I was ready to be back on my own turf once again. South Dakota is notorious for being windy and this particular day was no exception. The winds were wicked and not a battle I had anticipated. Traveling through 40-60 mph wind gusts, I got the sense that I was a vintage Bozo punching bag. Blasted on my side, bounced back, blasted again, mile over mile. Muscles tensed signaling me to work on letting go and join the wind. I tried desperately to hear my own words so often spoken to others: "Let the wind carry you. It's your companion." Yet again, I was blown into the opposing traffic lane only this time, there's actually oncoming traffic.

I was heading east on U.S. 14, a highway about as straight as they come. Traveling a straight road through windy prairies takes a lot of self-coaching. Late afternoon, I turned off the road to take a break in Pierre, 100 miles short of my intended destination for the day. It was time to make a decision. Keep going? Hang it up for the day? Set out early in the morning when the winds are usually calmer? After a little investigating with locals, I learned that the winds don't always recede in the morning in South Dakota. I was willing to take a chance on it. Decided to stop for the day and find a room.

I woke up at 4 a.m. to the clanging of the flag hooks against the metal pole at the end of the parking lot. A sense of dread set in. The wind had not subsided. I got out of bed to make myself a cup of tea and plan my escape route. I looked at my map and decided heading south to I-90 would be the fastest way to get out of South Dakota. I was willing to forego the scenery and adventure on U.S. 14 just to hurry up and be done with the wind, and South Dakota.

With a plan in place, I headed outside to sit on a bench and finish my tea. I sat listening to and feeling the wind encircling the peacefulness of predawn inactivity. As I drew the cup of steaming comfort to my lips, I noticed unexpected activity in the pitch black early morning sky. Lightning! Pink and purple bolts painted the sky in the west, north and south. I returned to my room to check the radar on the Weather Channel which completely changed my focus. The wind was no longer my biggest concern. Three storms were closing in and I needed to make a run for it. The tea was no longer a comfort. I dumped it, took a quick shower – determined it would be the only one I'd get that day. I hastily crammed my belongings into my saddlebags, twisted my earplugs snugly into place, threw a leg over the saddle, and fired up the bike. Feeling like the Lone Ranger, I jumped on U.S. 14 and headed blindly east into the darkened wilderness. Not another single human soul out there but me. I connected with my motorcycle and announced for all critters to move aside because I was coming through! I opened up the throttle feeling as though I was heading toward the edge of a cliff with the enemy in hot pursuit. I hammered down the road at 70+ mph. The wind was blasting at 40+ mph while spectacular displays of color illuminated my rearview mirrors as if they were movie screens. I was calmed by a sense of gratitude to be moving away from it all.

I traveled for more than an hour watching the movie in my rear-view mirrors fade away into the past. The horizon ahead began to illuminate with the promise of a spectacular sunrise. Under sunny skies, I traveled for the next 14 hours to my doorstep in Wisconsin. I arrived home just in time to watch the sun set from my own backyard.

Wake Up Call

Outside of Salt Lake City, Utah, on the road beyond Alta, there are spectacular views along a very narrow, winding, and poorly maintained road. It's the road's way of showing me that no matter how badly I want to keep looking outward, I still have to keep an eye on where I am now. At the end of the pavement was an overlook to Park City – the view spectacular, the energy empowering. I was on top of the world physically and figuratively, resonating with my surroundings. Below I could see a road continuing to Park City, a far more scenic route than going back through Salt Lake. It was a much slower and somewhat riskier way due to the descending, curvy, graveled road. Upon further investigation, I learned the gravel ended just a mile down, after which the pavement continued all the way into Park City. I've traveled mountain roads on gravel before. I knew I could handle this. Besides, it was way too beautiful to miss. Off I went.

First gear, second gear. The road began descending quickly toward a sharp curve. I decided I'd feel much more comfortable back in first gear. When I grabbed the clutch, I started losing the rear end of the bike while picking up momentum. Panic set in and escalated as a van came around the curve. I was headed straight into it. I'm certain the driver saw the color of my eyes as they suddenly felt bigger than my head.

Decision time. Ride over the edge? Run into the van? Lay the bike down? The second I surrendered to laying the bike down, the tension subsided. My shoulders relaxed and the hand that was unconsciously still gripping the clutch relaxed, giving me complete control of my motorcycle once again. I turned the bike back down the road, passing right by the van. The expressions on the faces inside were priceless. I couldn't help but laugh out loud at the message screaming in my head, "Let go of the wheel!" As I resumed breathing and realigned my focus, I lifted my head to a postcard view of the Salt Lake City landscape. There I was to receive it.

Freedom

I think of times I chose to ride instead of listening to fear tell me to sit it out. Those have been some of the best experiences of my life. During many of my roads trips, I've been approached by older men and women who chose not to ride when they had the calling. They didn't dance their dance, and now regret it. They've told me how they wish they'd done what I'm out there doing when they were my age. I can sense the passion they left dying in their hearts. I use that sense as fuel to keep going, to feed the desire of pursuing my passions, to give me the courage to push fear aside and just go. Danger isn't on the horizon or around the next curve. Life is!

Sometimes it's scary to dance your own dance. It can be a lonely place at times. Just when you feel you've taken a leap forward, you slam into a wall so hard it knocks you flat on your ass. You sit there asking yourself, "Why me?" "Why now?" "WHY!?"

There's something from the core of my being needing a voice – a voice overriding all the others from my past and present that tell me "You're not enough." Over and over again, I wake up to a new day and trust that I'm just not yet seeing the bigger picture – my heart tells me there is one and that's why I'm here.

The open road shows me again and again that the Universe has a way of pushing us to use our innermost strength to find the courage and the determination to move our self out of a rut or past a challenge. There is real comfort in knowing this.

"Your journey has molded you for your greater good, and it was exactly what it needed to be. Don't think that you've lost time. There is no short-cutting life. It took each and every situation you have encountered to bring you to now. And now is right on time." – Asha Tyson

Now That's What I Call a Joy Ride!

I get up in the morning to greet the sunrise, antici-pating the joy and adventure awaiting my senses on the open road. This is where my heart belongs. This is what my soul is longing for. As the sun rises into the sky, the shadows of nature begin to fade along with my own. The shadow self I have allowed to keep me from freedom, disap-pears as I twist the throttle and hit the road ready to open my heart once again.

I've been on the road, lost and alone, longing to find my way home. There appears to be such emptiness on those long stretches of highway. I find myself desperately seeking to fill the void I feel inside. I've let thoughts of the past and doubts of the future plague me to a point of being uncom-fortable and agitated with where I am.

Those self-sabotaging thoughts are no longer welcome on this ride. Regrets and unwanted thoughts of "not being enough" are left on the pavement. There isn't any room for excess baggage. It only slows down my traveling. I choose to twist the throttle in wide open spaces because I know that it opens a space within me to become more of who I truly am. It is in this space that I clearly see what feeds my soul. While the sun continues to rise and the shadows fade away, I can see the shadows are always smaller than the light which creates them.

There's no one out there talking, except me. No one asking questions and making demands, except me. There's no agenda to be followed other than the one I choose to impose upon myself. It's just me and the open road. I have found that what appears to be emptiness is indeed the space for my heart to open and my mind to let go. In this emptiness I can experience the joy my heart desires. In that empty place, nature has ways of reminding me that I am never truly alone.

Riding Home

By late November, winter settles in and riding days dwindle. I feel a little hole in my heart. I'm grateful for the sunshine warming my body as well as my soul because it's 41 degrees and I'm going for a ride. I suit up with all the cold gear I've got, throw a leg over my cold motorcycle and start her up. Misfire. Lucy, my motorcycle, has a little hole in her heart for this end of the season ritual, too. The engine chugs as the exhaust fumes waft through the crisp, cold air past my nose giving me a sweet adrenaline rush. The cold, hollow air makes the sound of the engine vibrate off of my neighbor's house. I feel it in every cell of my body. Blue sky above and a motorcycle between my legs grounding and connecting me to all I see, I am ready to take one last cruise for the season. As I enter the highway, the cold stings my face – the pain easily surpassed by the joy of the moment. I think about how much pain could be lessened or dismissed by simply surrendering to the moment – just letting it be exactly what it is.

Exhilarated and frozen, I return from my jaunt with a tear or two in my eyes. I tuck my bike away in the corner of the garage for its hibernation. I retreat to my dwelling to incorporate into my daily life what the road has taught me about life and living.

I have weathered many different types of storms. I've traversed hills, valleys, curves, and straight-of-ways, encountering roadblocks and dead ends along the way. Many roads have been beautiful while others have been down right frustrating to navigate. I've found twists and turns, as well as many surprises in my travels. Some have been blissful and exhilarating, others have left my heart in my stomach.

When I finally found the joy in getting lost, I realized what it means to ride free. Inherently, I always knew how to find my way home.

cs

I'd like to thank; my dear friend, Paul Z for introducing me to motorcycling and freedom of the open road, Koelle Simpson, for inspiring me to discover more of myself through the eyes of my iron horse, Meadow DeVor, for enlightening me to remove my windshield and ride WITH the wind, and most importantly, my two boys, Schuyler and Wyatt, for being my most inspiring teachers of life.

Karen Allen is a Certified Life Coach personally trained by Martha Beck, PhD. She spent the first 16 years of her career as an urban Special Education teacher, followed by

2 children and a divorce, after which she discovered the open road to be one of her greatest teachers of life. The knowledge, wisdom, and experience she acquired traveling 200,000 miles of North America, she shares with Life's lost and weary travelers seeking direction in finding their way home. Karen also conducts Medicine Rides: on-the-road workshops for motorcyclist seeking a deeper connection to, and appreciation for, themselves and all of life. Karen invites you to explore www.motorcyclemedicine.com

Ↄ

Bibliography

Works cited throughout the book:

Martha Beck

Martha Beck's work underlies our approach to coaching. She generously grants permission to her Certified Life Coaches to use, adapt, and build on her concepts. Her teaching influences us much more often than we specifically mention her. These resources are particularly good places to start:

Beck, M. (2001). *Finding Your Own North Star: Claiming the Life You Were Meant to Live.* New York, NY: Three Rivers Press.

Beck, M. (2003). *The Joy Diet: 10 Daily Practices for a Happier Life.* New York, NY: Crown Publishers

Beck, M. (2007). *The Four Day Win: End Your Diet War and Achieve Thinner Peace.* New York, NY: Rodale, Inc.

Beck, M. (2008). *Steering by Starlight: Find Your Right Life, No Matter What!* New York, NY: Rodale, Inc.

Her website: www.MarthaBeck.com

Byron Katie

The Work of Byron Katie is a profound means of investigating the truth of our thoughts. Essential references on The Work are:

Katie, B., & Mitchell, S. (2002). *Loving What Is: Four Questions That Can Change Your Life*. New York, NY: Harmony Books.

Website: www.TheWork.com

Works cited in specific chapters:

You've Just Been Elected to the Board:

Orman, S. (2009). *Suze Orman's 10 Tips for a Fresh Financial Start*. O, The Oprah Magazine, January 2009. New York, NY

Dominguez, J. and Robins, V. (1993). *Your Money or Your Life*. New York, NY: Penguin Group

Embracing Change:

Castillo, B. (2009). *Self Coaching 101*. Everett, WA: BookSurge Press.

Escape from Mini-Van Madness:

Castillo, B. (2009). *Self Coaching 101*. Everett, WA: BookSurge Press.

Stephens, S. and Gray, A. (2004). *The Worn Out Woman: When Your Life Is Full and Your Spirit is Empty*. Sisters, Oregon: Multnomah Publishers

Swenson, R.A. (1992). *Margin: Restoring Emotional, Physical, Financial and Time Reserves to Overloaded Lives*. Colorado Springs, Colorado: Navpress.

Warner, J. (2005). *Perfect Madness: Motherhood in the Age of Anxiety*. New York, NY: Riverhead Books.

From Tragedy to Transformation:

Hayes, S.C., Strosahl, K.D., & Wilson, K.G. (2003). *Acceptance and Commitment Therapy: An Experiential Approach to Behavior Change*. New York, NY: The Guilford Press.

Finally Write That Book!:

Block, Lawrence. (1981). *Telling Lies for Fun and Profit*. New York, NY: William Morrow and Company, Inc.

Castillo, B. (2009). *Self Coaching 101.* Everett, WA: BookSurge Press.

Website for the Emotional Freedom Technique: www.emofree.com

Practical Guide to Making Good Choices:

Day, Laura. *Welcome To Your Crisis*. Little, Brown and Company, 2007.

A Woman's Energy Crisis and the Essential Art of Self-Love:

Domar, A.D., & Dreher, H. (2000). *Self-Nurture: Learning to Care for Yourself as Effectively As You Care for Everyone Else*. New York, NY: Penguin Books.

Hayes, S.C., Strosahl, K.D., & Wilson, K.G. (2003). *Acceptance and Commitment Therapy: An Experiential*

Approach to Behavior Change. New York, NY: The Guilford Press.

Maw, J. (2009). *The Art of Self-Love: Your Essential Key to Successful Manifesting.* Salt Lake City, UT: Good Vibe Coaching (self-published e-Book)

Myss, C. (1997). *Anatomy of the Spirit: The Seven Stages of Power and Healing.* New York, NY: Three Rivers Press.

Richardson, C. (1999). *Take Time for Your Life: A Personal Coach's 7-Step Program for Creating the Life You Want.* New York, NY: Broadway Books.

Our Brain When We Grieve:

Braestrup, Reverend Kate (2007) *Here If You Need Me.* Little, Brown and Company

Fehmi, Les, and Robbins, Jim (2008) *The Open-Focus Brain: Harnessing the Power of Attention to Heal Mind and Body.* Trumpeter – www.openfocus.com

McWilliams, Peter, Bloomfield, H., and Colgrove, M. (1993) *How to Survive the Loss of a Love.* Prelude Press – www.mcwilliams.com or directly at www.mcwilliams.com/books/books

Neeld, Elizabeth Harper (2003) *Seven Choices: Finding Daylight After Loss Shatters Your World.* Grand Central Publishing – www.elizabethharperneeld.com

Nin, Anaïs *Risk* – www.anaisnin.com

Twain, Mark   *The Death of Jean* – Jalic, Inc., www.online-literature.com/twain/1316

Williams, M., Teasdale, J., Segal, Z., and Kabat-Zinn, J. (2007) *The Mindful Way through Depression: Freeing Yourself from Chronic Unhappiness.* The Guilford Press – www.mindfulnesstapes.com